Christine Nickl-Weller | Hans Nickl (eds.)

Hospital
Architecture

BRAUN

CONTENTS

CONTENTS

Contemporary Hospital Design
by Prof. Hans Nickl and Prof. Christine Nickl-Weller

Comfortable, serene and relaxing are not terms that one necessarily associates with illness. However, it is exactly these words that should be evoked by healthcare facilities. The comparison with a cherished holiday home, first made by the architecture critic Katharina Matzig in reference to the Agatharied hospital, demonstrates that modern hospital architecture is quite capable of creating locations that cater to patients' well-being and enjoyment, providing them with an opportunity to forget their illnesses.

The international projects exhibited in this volume demonstrate a diverse understanding of hospitals as places of healing. In the first instance, this internationalism facilitates a direct and therefore exciting comparison between the various projects. How will the countries in this volume approach

↖ | **Jacobo Pontormo: Life in Hospital,** 1514, Fresco, 91 × 150 cm, Galleria dell'Accademia, Florence. This picture originates from the Hospital San Matteo in Florence and symbolizes the Caritas, who supported the construction of ecclesiastical hospitals, since the Council of Nicaea (325 A.D.).
← | **J.C. Woudanus based on a drawing by W. Swanenburg: Anatomical Theater,** 1610, engraving, 32.6 × 39.5 cm, 1610, detail. This anatomical theater was built under order of Pieter Pauw in Leiden, 1596. This enlightened strategy lead to significant advancement, particularly in terms of surgical techniques. The skeletons of Adam and Eve with an apple tree can be seen in the foreground.

the topic of hospital architecture? What challenges exist? What position does hospital architecture occupy today and how will it tackle increasingly complex challenges and the rapid changes facing modern society? And finally, how will modern hospital planning satisfy the growing needs and demands of the user, patients and personnel? To enable architects to tackle the challenges facing healthcare architecture, the first question that must be considered concerns the influential factors.

Perhaps the most important change taking place involves the role of a hospital: hospital operators need to move away from being purely care-oriented organizations and develop into actual businesses that can compete as a service provider.

Even technical and pharmacological medical developments are advancing at such a rapid pace that some areas gain an entirely new meaning, while their long-established predecessors simply cease to exist. This can be seen most clearly in the effects of new technologies, such as keyhole surgery and the increasing short recovery time spent in hospital.

The changing demographic of our society has resulted in new disease patterns that are gaining in importance and inevitably result in new healthcare challenges. The differentiation between nursing and therapy, for example, perfectly demonstrates the changing demands of an aging society. Our society is changing rapidly, many of the assumptions and experiences that have always been taken for granted are now being questioned and examined; yet it is exactly this that brings about exciting challenges and offers new opportunities in terms of planning buildings and healthcare institutions.

As architects, it is our opinion that the only way to successfully accomplish these complex tasks is to utilize high-quality architectural design that emphasizes structural elements. The quality of the architecture alone makes it possible for the general public to identify "their" hospital. It is only under these conditions that such buildings will once more acquire their own identity and become pillars of the community.

The subject of health in today's society is just as ubiquitous as the appearance of the built environment. The quality of

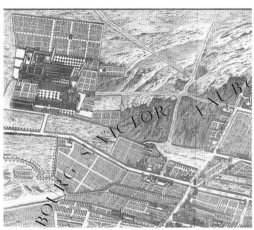

urban development and architecture will shape tomorrow's world. This brings with it a certain responsibility, as does the design of socially important high-quality, healthy spaces that will meet the requirements of our cultural and aesthetic demands.

It is quickly becoming clear that the hospital represents far more than the simple fulfillment of technical standards and functions. Of far greater importance is the creation of an environment that can offer support to those in need, regardless of race or culture, aiding them in their recovery and helping them to remain healthy in the future.

Modern hospital architecture, and in particular the projects represented in this book, must pursue the following important questions: How can architecture contribute to the healing process? Or: Which influences do the built and natural environments have on the perception of healthy people, and how can they remain healthy?

The factors that play a role in this change according to the individual nature of each project; but there are key areas, which must always be examined anew, including natural light and ventilation, colors, economical functions and harmony with the environment.

However, the most important approach is the development of regulatory structures, which place people at the center of all considerations and plans. This means the creation of a place, a space in the city, which must support and strengthen the active and empowered patients of the future, while simultaneously providing employees with an appropriate environment and functioning as a valuable component for the entire population of a city. The goal of all these considerations is to improve the quality of healthcare facilities through the development of an architecture that caters to the needs of the population and promotes recovery. However, the benefits are not only economical, high-quality architecture also makes a valuable contribution to society and to our modern-day culture.

↖↖↖| **Jost Amman: The Barber Surgeon,** 1568, woodcut from "Das Ständebuch". The barber surgeons, along with the anatomists, were organized into guilds relatively early on. They were assigned various tasks that are today undertaken by doctors or alternative practitioners – cupping can be seen in this picture.

↖↖ | **Matthäus Seutter: The Large Royal Military Hospital or the Charité,** approx. 1740, colorized etching. Numerous infirmaries later became hospitals; such as the Berlin plague house from 1710.

↖ | **Libéral Bruant: Hospital chapel of La Salpêtrière, Paris,** approx. 1675. This former gunpowder factory was converted to a poorhouse, served as prison for prostitutes, and simultaneously as an institute for the criminally insane and epileptics. At the end of the 18th century it was the largest hospital in the world, with a capacity of 10,000 patients plus 300 prisoners. In the 19th century it became the birthplace of modern neurology.

↑ | **Claude Lucas based on drawings by Louis Bretez: Turgot map of Paris,** 1739, engraving on 21 plates 250.2 × 322.5 cm. The isometric plan shows the Hôtel des Invalides still located outside the urban area.

↗ | **Libéral Bruant and Jules Hardouin-Mansart: Hôtel des Invalides, Paris,** 1676. Residential hospitals for war invalids and soldiers who were no longer able to work were a predecssor for hospital buildings.

→ | **Rembrandt: The Anatomy Lesson of Dr. Nicolaes Tulp,** 1632, Oil on canvas, 216.5 × 169.5 cm, Mauritshuis, The Hague. In the 17th century anatomy was not an exact science and sometimes even served as a form of entertainment – the forerunner of modern television programs like Grey's Anatomy and CSI. The painting portrays the public dissection of an executed criminal; the only event of its kind to take place in that year in Amsterdam.

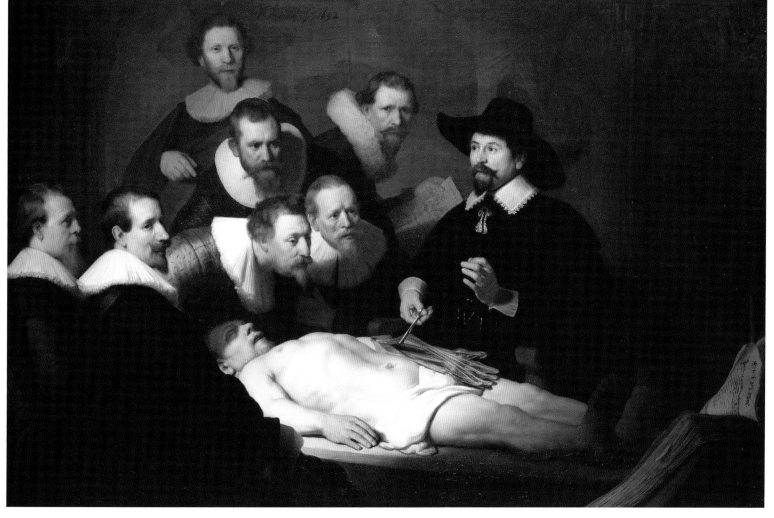

People from different backgrounds have different demands and conventions. This fact is demonstrated by the varying architectural examples, which clearly cater to cultural influences. The impossibility of separating society and culture from the subject of health and well-being demonstrates that the hospital itself represents one of the most important facilitators of social coexistence.

Furthermore, the subject of healthcare has long since occupied a central position in our collective public consciousness. We live in a society strongly characterized by individualism, where each individual must determine his or her own fate. We want to remain able-bodied for as long as possible, to enable us to participate in the rapid developments of our society and culture. Our sense of responsibility for our own well-being and health has increased dramatically. Care of the human body, the fear of illness, of getting older, of being different, of becoming incapable and of an existence on the periphery of our experience-oriented and rapidly changing society, are factors that heavily influence – albeit subconsciously – our daily existence.

Moreover, we live in the information age, an era where almost everybody has round-the-clock access to a wealth of information and knowledge. Personal health can be reviewed assessed and evaluated at any time. This has created an ever-increasing demand for provisional healthcare. Health equates freedom in this era of individualism. Modern man has become embedded in a health-oriented culture where the main task is to seek out disorders, classify and ultimately to eliminate them. As a result of this, a more holistic understanding of internal and exterior correlations is being lost; for example, the consideration of the individual as part of the whole, social psychological and mental aspects. Location plays a particularly important role in this.

The hospital plays a special role as an important component of the urban fabric

↖ | **Canaletto: Royal Hospital for Seamen,** approx. 1753, oil on canvas, 66 × 112.5 cm, National Maritime Museum, Greenwich. This military hospital was built according to plans by Christopher Wren. Building work began in Greenwich in 1696 and the construction is considered to be the forerunner of both the pavilion and comb-type hospital building structures.
↑ | **Carl Gotthard Langhans: Anatomical Theater, Berlin,** 1790. This is the oldest remaining academic teaching building in Berlin. Medical training became much more systematic during the 18th/19th centuries.
↗ | **Ilja Repin: The Surgeon Evgueni Vasilievich Pavlov in the Operating Theater,** 1888, oil on canvas. 27.8 × 40.3 cm, State Tretyakov Gallery, Moscow. Diethylether was first used as an anaesthetic by the dentist William Thomas Green Morton in 1846.
→ | **Kurt Diestel and Georg Thür: Charité, Berlin,** 1917. By the end of the 19th century Berlin hospital was extended to a 133,000-square-meter campus, located on the outskirts of the city's urban development.
→→| **Lluís Domènech i Montaner: Hospital de la Santa Creu i Sant Pau, Barcelona,** from 1902. This large campus is one of the world's most exuberantly decorated hospitals. It is built in the Catalonian Modernism style and is a UNESCO site.

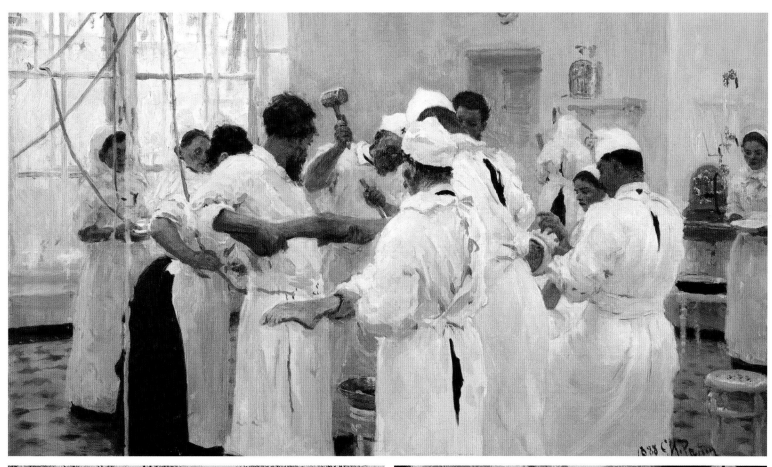

and therefore occupies a special position in society. It is for this reason that it must meet particularly high quality requirements. One of the fundamental objectives of this book is to present this demand for excellence across the whole healthcare spectrum, from small practices to specialized clinics to large institutions.

However, the aim is not only to display the projects, but rather to provoke further thought and discussion. Which trends are obvious, which developments are recognizable and how should these be interpreted in terms of future challenges and changes? And finally: an evaluation of these trends allows us to draw conclusions regarding the examples shown in terms of questions like: what functions well and what will change or develop further in the future. However heterogeneous, diverse and multifaceted the various approaches to planning and health facilities may be, all the projects presented in this book show a high degree of quality consciousness, which, in our experience, legitimates

the strict demands placed on this area of architecture.

In this sense, the main aim of this book is to provoke thought and inspire excitement, to promote future demands and expectations of high-quality architecture and to further develop innovative visions.

↖↖ | **Martin-Pierre Gauthier: Hôpital Lariboisière, Paris,** 1854. The construction of single pavilions connected by walkways became a popular building style during the 19th century. This type of architecture reduced the risk of infection and provided better ventilation.

↖ | **Vincent van Gogh: Ward in the Hospital in Arles,** 1889, oil on canvas, 74 x 92 cm, collection of Oskar Reinhart, Winterthur. Bedrooms with numerous beds, separated from each other by just a curtain; this organization is still used today in various countries around the world.

↑ | **Jan Duiker with Bernard Bijvoet and Jan Gerko Wiebenga: Sanatorium Zonnestraal, Hilversum,** 1931. By the end of the 19th century sanatoriums introduced a new terraced form of hospital architecture, which took its example from beach resorts.

↗ | **Lluís Domènech i Montaner: Hospital de la Santa Creu i Sant Pau, Barcelona,** from 1902. These 48 planned pavilions were constructed in two building phases; the first completed in 1911 and the second in 1930. Connecting walkways and all technical facilities are located underground.

→ | **Alvar Aalto: Sanatorium, Paimio,** 1932. This building is a UNESCO World Heritage Site and, according to the architect, should be viewed as a medical instrument in the fight against tuberculosis; a disease that can be banished by fresh air and sunlight. The architecture also encompassed the entire interior design.

→→| **Erhardt Gißke: High-rise ward, the Charité, Berlin,** 1982. High-rise hospitals first appeared in the 1930s. This example in East Berlin, in close proximity to the Berlin wall, served as a status symbol against the West during the Cold War. Of the 21 stories, the 17 uppermost house the hospital wards.

GENERAL HOSPITAL

↑ | **Main view,** at dusk in winter
→ | **Façade,** detail

CircleBath Hospital

Bath

CircleBath is Foster + Partners' first hospital and represents a radical departure from orthodox approaches to hospital planning. The three-story building is set into the hills on the edge of a protected green belt. The building will house operating rooms, bedrooms, consultation, treatment and recovery spaces. The hospital is planned around a central light-filled atrium, which forms the focus for patients, staff and visitors, with private consultation rooms leading from it at ground level and inpatient bedrooms arranged around it above. The northern façade comprises dark paneling at the lower levels, while on the south, extensive glazing opens out to views over the surrounding rolling countryside. Appearing to float above this recessive skirting, the rectangular upper volume and roof, enclosing all 28 bedrooms, is clad in a reflective lattice of aluminum shingles.

PROJECT FACTS

Address: Foxcote Avenue, Peasedown St John, Bath BA2 8SQ, United Kingdom. **Client:** Circle Partnership. **Completion:** 2009. **Gross floor area:** 6,367 m². **Main materials:** wood acoustic panels, glass. **Type:** general hospital. **Building:** new construction. **Treatment areas:** operating rooms, treatment rooms, recovery spaces. **Operator:** private.

↑ | **Lobby**, information
↙ | **Ground floor plan**

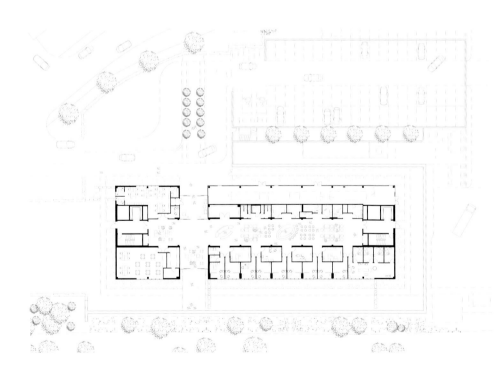

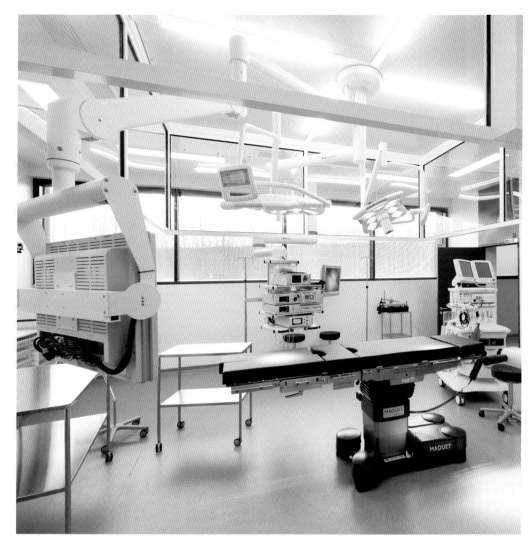

← | **Operating room**
↓ | **Section**

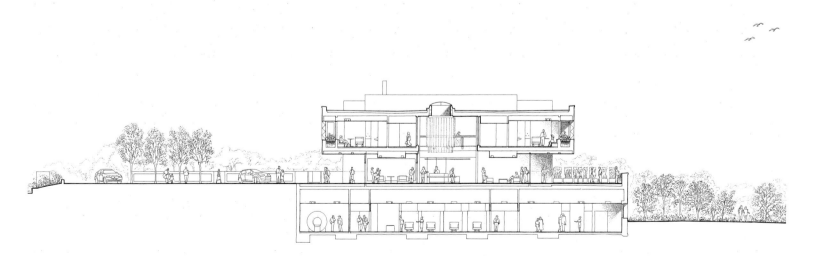

Zeidler Partnership
Architects

↑ | **New entrance plaza**
→ | **Entrance lobby**

Juravinski Hospital

Hamilton

The Juravinski Hospital Redevelopment is Hamilton's largest healthcare project to date: 39,484 square meters of new construction and 3,252 square meters of renovated space. The first phase of renewal focused on the most critical departments, including diagnostic imaging, surgery, emergency and a component of beds. The architectural challenge was to add new areas and facilitate renovated space on a crowded site while organizing 13 buildings and two parking structures built in an ad hoc manner over seven decades – all into a cohesive healthcare facility. The resulting designs improved wayfinding, rationalized flow of patients, staff and visitors and created a welcoming and universally accessible front entrance. Bridging critical departmental adjacencies created an operationally seamless environment, i.e. emergency areas adjacent to diagnostic imagining and medical decision unit, intensive care unit adjacent to surgery. The emergency department's innovative open design boasts a number of features that modernize the space and ensure it is suited to the unique needs of emergency care.

Address: 711 Concession Street, Hamilton, ON L5V 1C3, Canada. **Client:** Henderson General Hospital/ Hamilton Health Sciences. **Completion:** 2012. **Gross floor area:** 39,484 m². **Co-architects:** Garwood Jones + Hanham. **Main materials:** glass, steel, concrete. **Type:** general hospital. **Building:** new construction, renovation. **Treatment areas:** operating rooms. **Operator:** state.

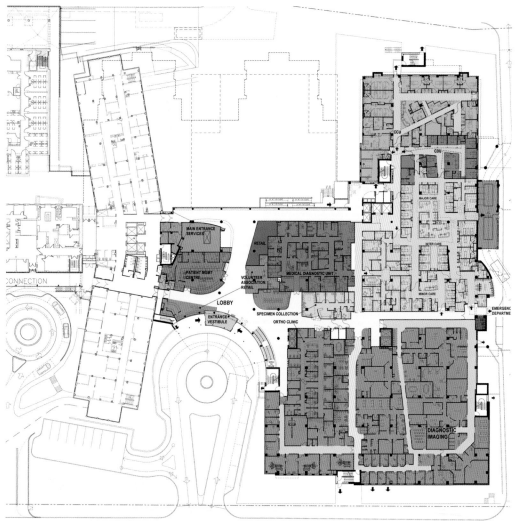

←← | **Exterior**, facing the escarpment

↖ | **Redevelopment ground floor plan**, phase one

↓ | **Patient room**

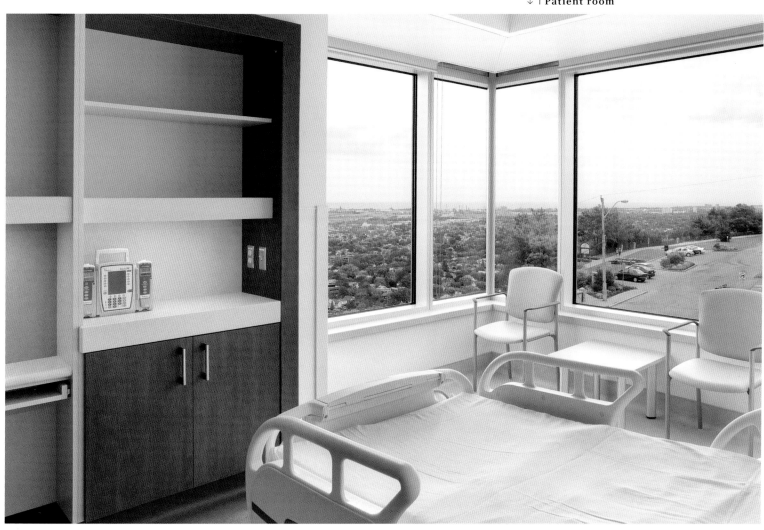

Pei Cobb Freed & Partners

↑ | Exterior
→ | Atrium detail

Jacobi Medical Center
Ambulatory Care Pavilion

New York City

The centerpiece of a master plan to modernize the fifty-year-old Jacobi hospital campus, this ambulatory care pavilion joins the existing facility in an extensive landscape of mature trees. The new building extends the exceptional environmental qualities of the campus, incorporating a garden courtyard and atrium space curved to offer a sweeping view of sky and garden, while the transparent facade reflects the layered, leafy context. Public circulation and waiting areas overlook the landscape. Clinical areas are tied into medical spaces in the existing structure, with an emphasis on horizontal continuity of departments. Inpatient, outpatient, and diagnostic facilities are woven together in a rigorously planned tapestry of associated uses.

Address: 1400 Pelham Parkway South, Bronx, New York City, NY 10461, USA. **Client:** Dormitory
Authority of the State of New York. **Completion:** 2008. **Gross floor area:** 11,799 m² (new building),
4,181 m² (renovation). **Associate architect:** daSilva Architects. **Main materials:** Deer Isle granite,
brick, travertine, glass, stainless steel. **Type:** general hospital. **Building:** new construction, renovation.
Treatment areas: operating rooms. **Operator:** state.

←← | **Night view,** of exterior
↑ | **Atrium**
↓ | **Section**

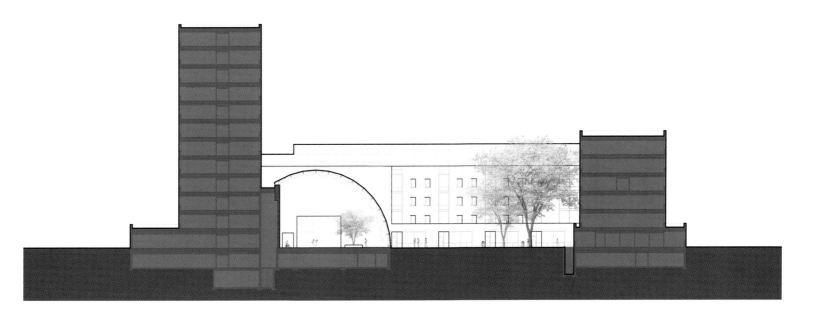

↑ | **Building volume,** in landscaped surroundings
→ | **Palomar Medical Center,** represents the most advanced methods of hospital architecture

Palomar Medical Center

Escondido

CO Architects conceptualized a functional and flexible vertical garden hospital set within a garden campus configuration. The signature patient tower building figuratively opens its arms to welcome patients. A vertical garden at the center of the south façade overlooks the extensive landscaped roof and garden terraces. Natural light streams into surgery and recovery areas – something seldom seen in US hospitals. In addition to influx of natural light throughout the building, CO Architects instituted several features to make PMC exemplary of sustainable health care design. Site planning, landscape, non-institutional architectural expression, and material selection are all strongly influenced by the desire to merge nature and building.

Address: 2185 West Citracado Parkway, Escondido, CA 92029, USA. **Client:** Palomar Health. **Completion:** 2012. **Gross floor area:** 68,377 m². **Structural engineers:** KPFF Consulting Engineers. **Landscape architects:** Spurlock Poirier. **Main materials:** fiber-reinforced concrete panels, glass, solid panel, corrugated and perforated metal. **Type:** general hospital. **Building:** new construction. **Treatment areas:** operating rooms, rehabilitation. **Operator:** state.

↑ | **Entrance**, front view
← | **Ground floor plan**

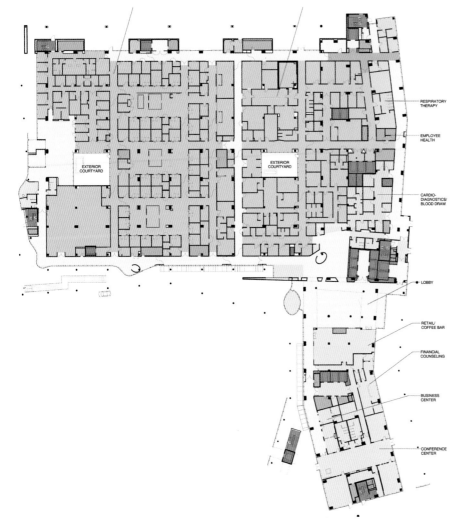

RESPIRATORY
THERAPY

EMPLOYEE
HEALTH

EXTERIOR
COURTYARD

EXTERIOR
COURTYARD

CARDIO-
DIAGNOSTICS/
BLOOD DRAW

LOBBY

RETAIL/
COFFEE BAR

FINANCIAL
COUNSELING

BUSINESS
CENTER

CONFERENCE
CENTER

← | **Expansive windows line outer hall-ways,** allowing for abundant natural light
↓ | **Outdoor gardens,** bring natural light and views to waiting areas

Nickl & Partner Architekten

↑ | **Hospital with main entrance**
→ | **View of forecourt,** from glazed main
entrance

General Hospital

Yingkou

The Yingkou General Hospital is located in a district of Yingkou in north-east China. The
design of the new building reflects the dynamics of the location, situated in a continu-
ously growing and changing city. The dynamically folded volume is positioned above a
base and is oriented toward the south, a design feature that provides ideal interior spatial
conditions. The large, bright entrance hall is connected to the main access corridor and
boasts numerous plants and water features; bringing the outside inside. Natural lighting
and ventilation techniques also reflect the desire to create a light and natural interior.

PROJECT FACTS

Address: Haiping Road 3, Liaoning, Yingkou, Bayuquan, China. **Client:** Yingkou General Hospital. **Completion:** 2010. **Gross floor area:** 70,000 m². **Local general planner:** Liaoning Provincial Building Design & Research Institute. **Main materials:** natural stone, glass, façade light installation. **Type:** general hospital. **Building:** new construction. **Treatment areas:** operating rooms, rehabilitation, water therapy, physiotherapy. **Operator:** state.

↑ | **Detail,** façade light installation shines out at dusk
↙ | **Section**

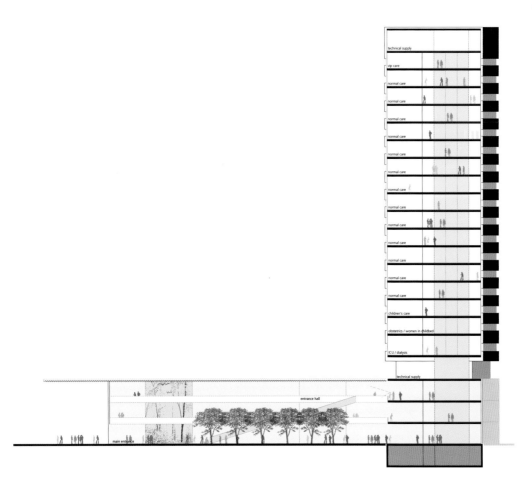

← | **Connecting bridge,** with characteristic glass roof
↓ | **Site plan**

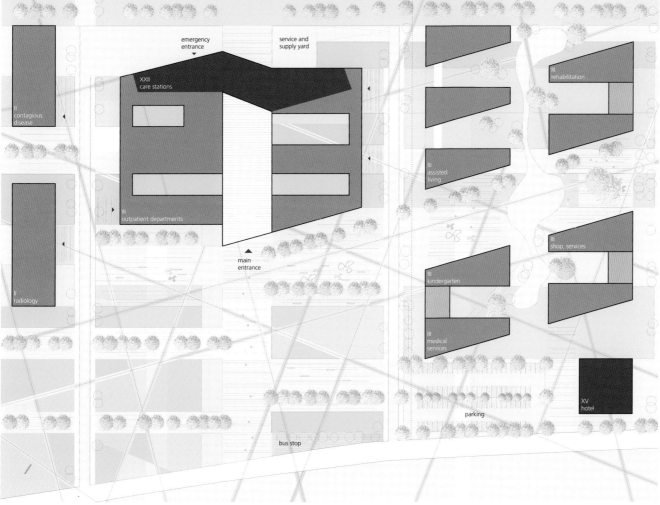

Clark/Kjos Architects
GBJ Architecture

↑ | Lobby
→ | Waiting area

MultiCare Good Samaritan Hospital Dally Tower

Puyallup

Dally Tower puts the patient at the center of the care process. The design creates a therapeutic patient experience through simplified access, emphasis on natural light, an abundance of natural wood finishes, artwork GBJ four therapeutic gardens. In the patient units, dedicated zones are provided in private patient rooms for family members, each with abundant natural light and garden or mountain view. Decentralized staff stations keep caregivers close to patients in inpatient and diagnostic areas. Dally Tower symbolizes the hospital's new status as regional medical center, with tower and garden overlooking the city. As the first inpatient hospital in Washington state to be awarded LEED Gold for sustainability, it expresses community health leadership.

Address: 401 15th Avenue SE, Puyallup, WA 98372, USA. **Client:** MultiCare Good Samaritan Hospital. **Completion:** 2011. **Gross floor area:** 34,467 m². **Main materials:** concrete and steel frame, brick, steel panel, curtainwall exterior finishes. **Type:** general hospital. **Building:** new construction. **Operator:** private.

↑ | **Entrance,** at night
↓ | **Third floor plan**

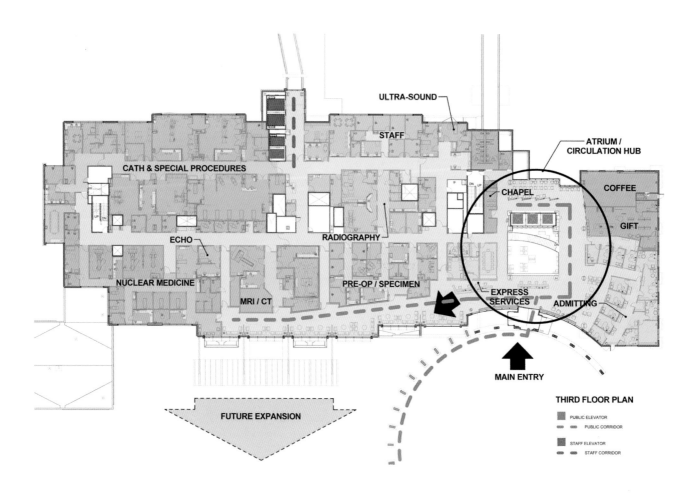

ULTRA-SOUND

STAFF

ATRIUM / CIRCULATION HUB

CATH & SPECIAL PROCEDURES

CHAPEL

COFFEE

GIFT

ECHO

RADIOGRAPHY

NUCLEAR MEDICINE

PRE-OP / SPECIMEN

EXPRESS SERVICES

ADMITTING

MRI / CT

MAIN ENTRY

FUTURE EXPANSION

THIRD FLOOR PLAN

PUBLIC ELEVATOR
PUBLIC CORRIDOR
STAFF ELEVATOR
STAFF CORRIDOR

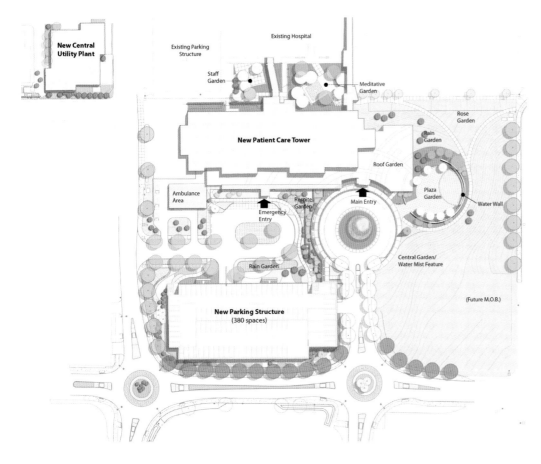

↖ | Site plan
↓ | Entrance canopy

↑ | **Glazed walkways,** creating new shortcuts and optimize logistics
→ | **New treatment wings,** ensuring functionality and flexibility of historic hospital

Gentofte Hospital Extension

Hellerup

The aim of the extension of Gentofte Hospital was to update the hospital and optimize logistics. The intention was to insert a modern core into the original complex and renovate and modernize the existing buildings. The hospital's outpatient departments are located on the ground floor along with the information and waiting areas, a strategy that vastly improves the clarity of the layout. On the uppermost levels, the new area houses the most equipment-heavy rooms, such as 24 new operating rooms, while on the equivalent stories, the older buildings are utilized as inpatient wards. This layout minimizes transport needs. To preserve the character of the 1920s brick buildings, the new area has light façades clad in satin glass.

Address: Niels Andersens Vej 65, 2900 Hellerup, Denmark. **Client:** The Capital Region of Denmark. **Completion:** 2009. **Gross floor area:** 15,000 m². **Main materials:** concrete, glass façades. **Type:** general hospital. **Building:** new construction. **Staff areas:** offices, changing rooms. **Treatment areas:** operating rooms. **Operator:** state.

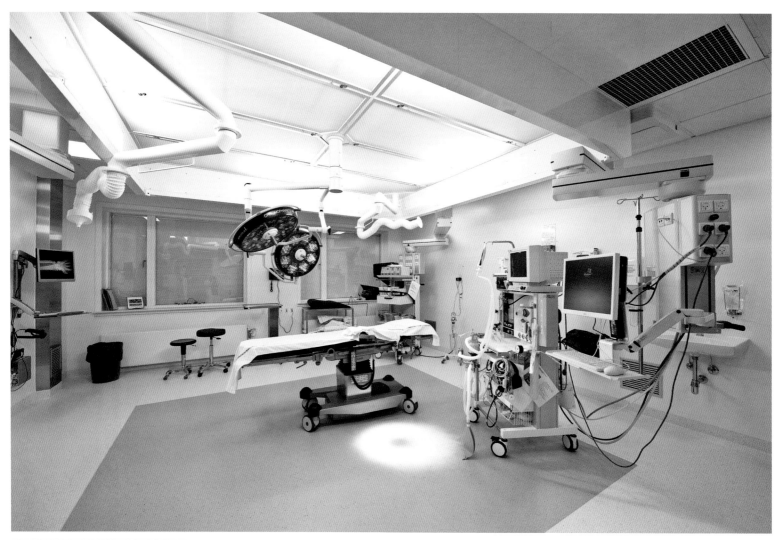

↑ | **Treatment room,** radiotherapy
← | **Interior,** café and information area

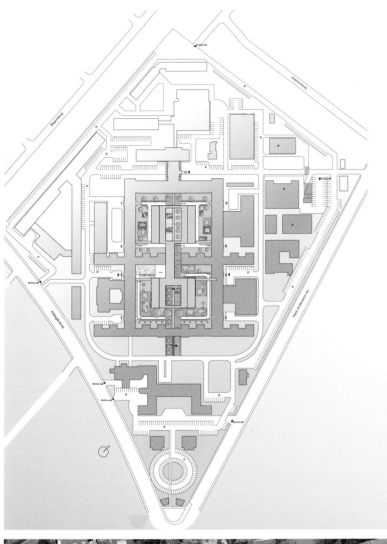

↖ | Site plan
↓ | Bird's-eye view

↑ | **South-east view,** horizontal paneling projects over façade
→ | **Entrance,** cantilevered building volume

Cardiovascular Center

Nuremberg

This cardiovascular center at the Nuremberg South Clinic houses state-of-the-art cardiology medicine and vascular surgery operation technology. The interdisciplinary networking of cardiology, vascular surgery, heart surgery and diagnostics into a logical spatial sequence results in a new kind of examination and treatment procedure. The new two-story building is modest in design, retreating behind the more dominating original building of the south clinic (1984–1994), thus preserving the urban appearance of the building and lines of sight. The horizontal paneling projects out slightly over the façades and establishes a dialogue with the existing care building and its design code. The atriums and the orthogonal order of the exterior are continued by the interior design.

Address: Breslauer Straße 201, 90471 Nuremberg, Germany. **Client:** Klinikum Nürnberg, Eigenbetrieb der Stadt Nürnberg. **Completion:** 2011. **Gross floor area:** 3,800 m². **Main materials:** reinforced concrete skeleton structure, post and rail type façade, Alucobond façade, greenery. **Type:** general hospital. **Building:** new construction. **Treatment areas:** operating rooms. **Operator:** state.

← | **Waiting area,** filled with natural light from
atrium
↓ | **Ground floor plan**

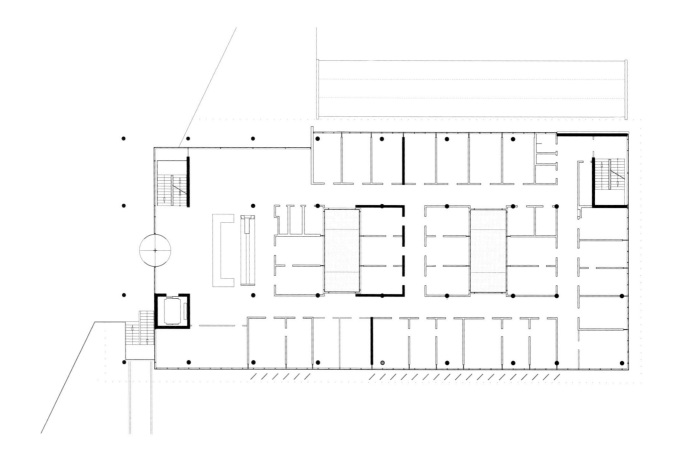

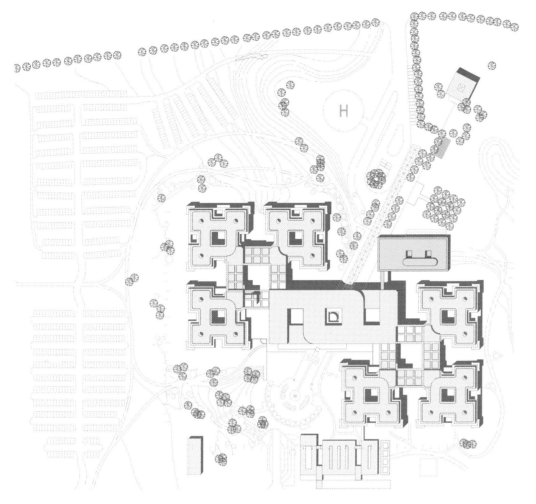

← | **Site plan**
↓ | **Light-filled space,** leading to operating rooms

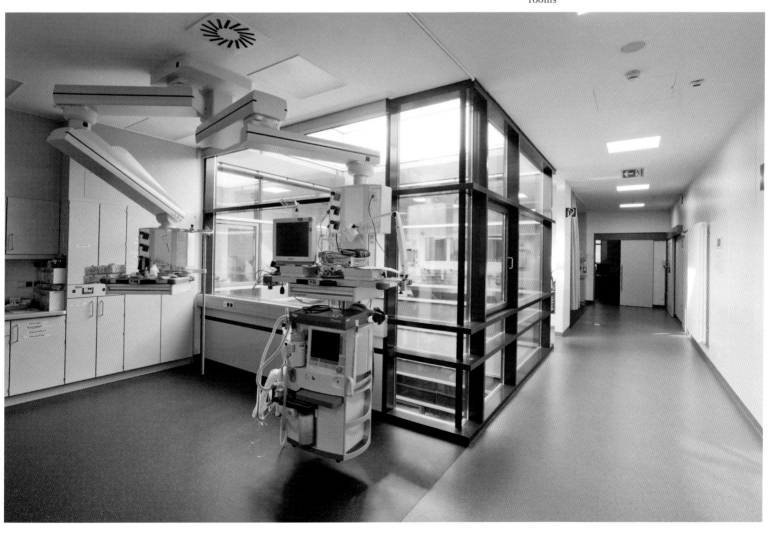

↑ | **Detail,** façade
↗ | **Main façade,** from roundabout
→ | **Main hall**

Esperit Sant Hospital Foundation

Santa Coloma de Gramenet

This hospital has a 240-bed capacity and 390 parking spaces laid out on five floors. In order to reduce the impact of its height and scale, the building is articulated into three clearly differentiated parts: a three-story plinth and two separate bodies, which are set at an angle, and are parallel to the streets. Together these accommodate the three basic functions that are now central and general services, inpatient and outpatient care. Formally, the ceramic cladding of their façades differentiates the plinth and the east and west buildings. The triangular area created between the two blocks is a covered public space which provides access to the hospital.

Address: Av. Mossén Pons i Rabadà s/n, 08923 Santa Coloma de Gramenet, Spain. **Client:** Fundació Hospital de l'Esperit Sant. **Completion:** 2007. **Gross floor area:** 38,681 m². **Main materials:** porcelain stoneware tiles, PVC. **Type:** general hospital. **Building:** new construction. **Treatment areas:** operating rooms, rehabilitation, water therapy, physiotherapy. **Operator:** private. **Signage:** room numbers integrated into flooring and walls.

↑ | Hallway
↙ | Ground floor plan
↓ | Section

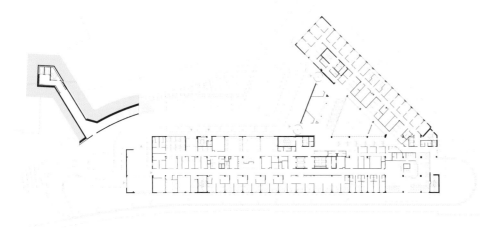

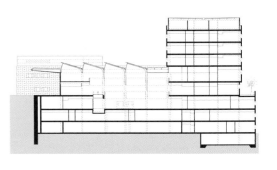

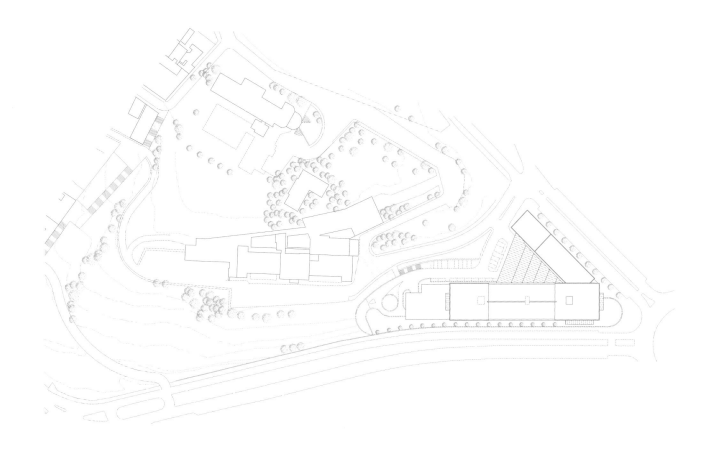

↑ | Site plan
↓ | Inpatient control room

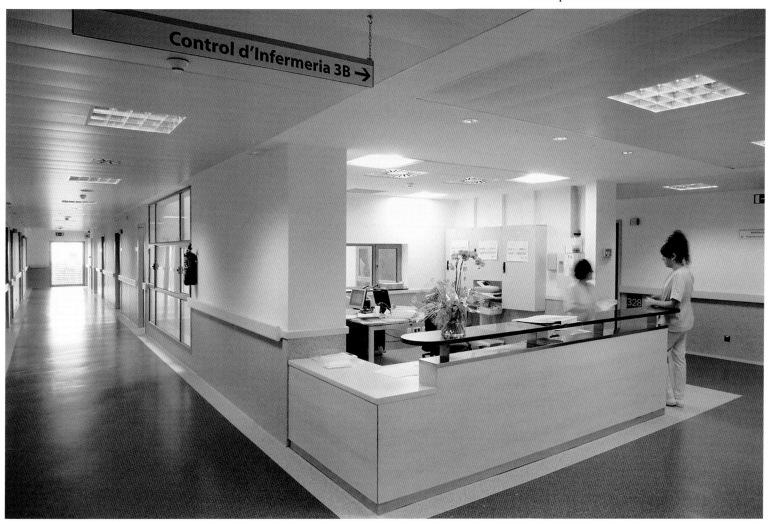

RRP
architekten + ingenieure

↑ | **Health center, view** from the lake
↗ | **Entrance**

RoMed Clinic – Renovation and Structural Improvements

Prien am Chiemsee

The Prien Clinic occupies a picturesque location near the Chiemsee freshwater lake in Bavaria, at the foot of the Alps and with views of the Herrenchiemsee castle. The master plan from RRP envisioned three building phases. The health center was built during the first building phase in 2009. The new building houses two modern outpatient operating rooms, connected to the existing surgery departments and sterile supply areas. Various doctors' practices are located on the first floor. Rehabilitation facilities with a terrace are located at lake level facing the sailing marina. Private care wards with views of the lake are located on the two upper levels. Views of the lake, sailing marina and the Alps make this location unique.

Address: Harrasser Straße 61–63, 83209 Prien am Chiemsee, Germany. **Client:** Kliniken der Stadt und des Landkreises Rosenheim GmbH. **Completion:** 2009. **Gross floor area:** 4,199 m². **Main materials:** exterior insulation finishing system. **Type:** general hospital. **Building:** new construction. **Treatment areas:** operating rooms, rehabilitation, physiotherapy. **Operator:** state.

↑ | **View of the Chiemsee,** from bedroom
↙ | **Ground floor plan**

← | **Wet room**
↓ | **Patient rooms,** with view of lake

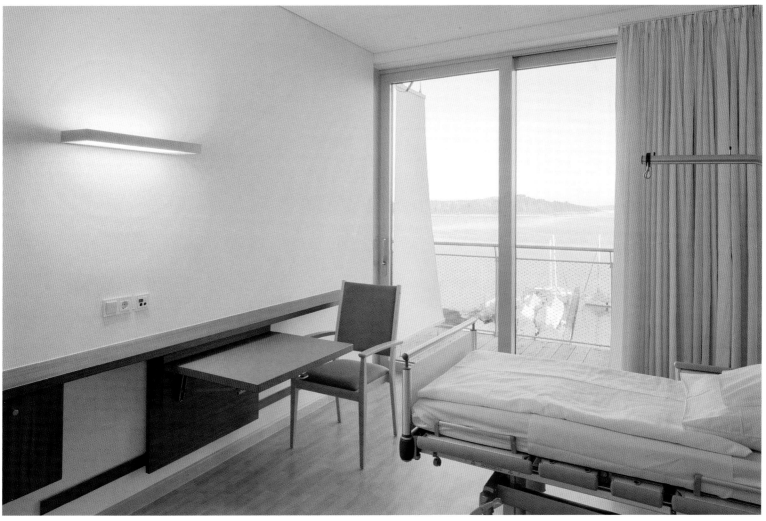

Stephan Höhne
Gesellschaft von Architekten

↑ | **Entrance,** emergency department
→ | **Lobby**

Friedrichshain Hospital

Berlin

The old ward, characterized by its classical architecture, has been extended by this integrated H-shaped ensemble. This design strategy brings the old and new buildings together to form a unified whole. While the new ward continues the six-story structure of the existing building, a three-story functional wing is oriented toward the street and serves as a new gatehouse. This acts as the central distribution point and also houses the three-story entrance lobby. The new emergency department with new operating rooms and intensive care ward extend the main building. This new building component fits seamlessly into the existing structure. A second clearly accentuated emergency entrance has been positioned adjacent to the main entrance.

PROJECT FACTS

Address: Landsberger Allee 49, 10249 Berlin, Germany. **Client:** Vivantes Berlin. **Completion:** 2011.
Gross floor area: 21,000 m². **Main materials:** brick. **Type:** general hospital. **Building:** new construction,
renovation. **Treatment areas:** physiotherapy. **Operator:** state.

↑ | Courtyard
↙ | Site plan
↓ | Ground floor plan

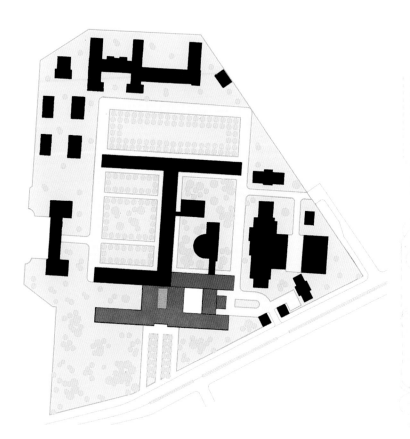

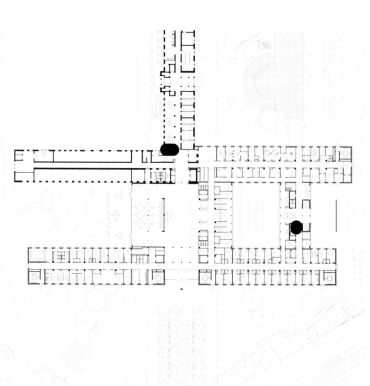

↑ | **Section and elevation**
↓ | **Interior,** emergency department

↑ | **Five-story long term care department**
↗ | **Main entrance,** courtyard
→ | **Circulation,** main access corridor

District Clinics Esslingen

Nürtingen

Intended as a replacement for the existing hospital, the new building with 331 general care and 18 intensive care beds was completed by the end of 2010. The new hospital building comprises an examination and treatment department with six operating rooms and intensive care ward, an emergency room and the separate areas housing surgery, diagnostic radiology, internal medicine, gynecology, maternity, laboratories and the five-story long-term care department with two care wards on each level, as well as the entrance hall with patient service center (PSC), café, kiosk, prayer room, administration offices, as an axis linking all the main departments with each other on short ways. Intelligent utilization of the sloping site gives the entrance a more "human scale", while simultaneously providing the patient rooms with attractive views of the Swabian Jura.

Address: Auf dem Säer 1, 72622 Nürtingen, Germany. **Client:** Landkreis Esslingen – Kreiskliniken Esslingen. **Completion:** 2010. **Gross floor area:** 37,800 m². **Main materials:** reinforced concrete, plaster, glass-aluminum façade. **Type:** general hospital. **Building:** new construction. **Treatment areas:** patient service center (PSC), emergency, surgery, diagnostic radiology, internal medicine, gynecology, maternity, laboratories. **Operator:** state.

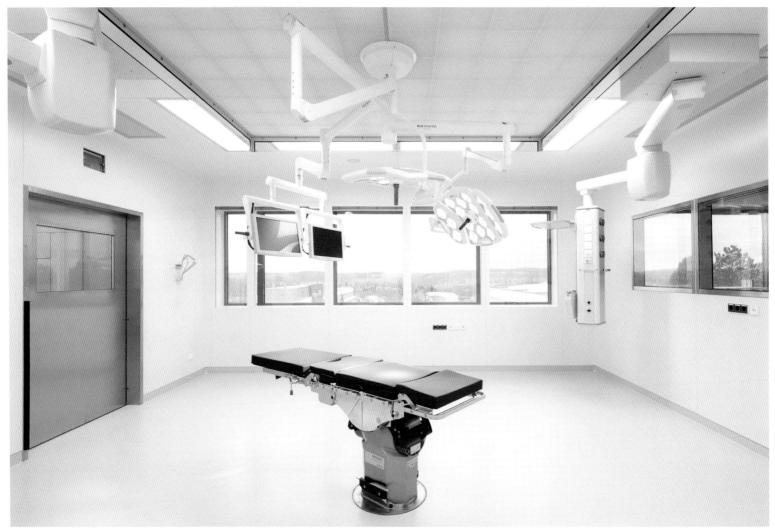

↑ | **Operating room,** with view to the outside
↙ | **Aerial view**

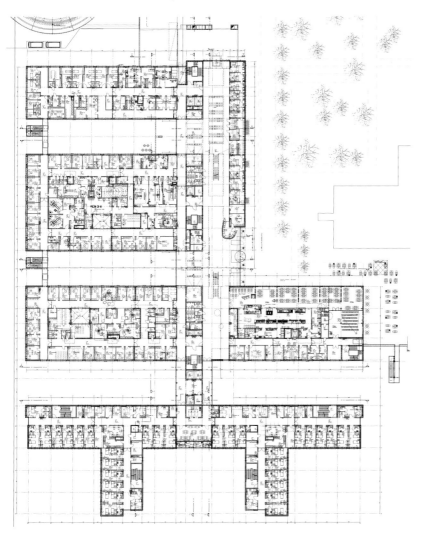

← | Entry level plan
↓ | Intensive care ward

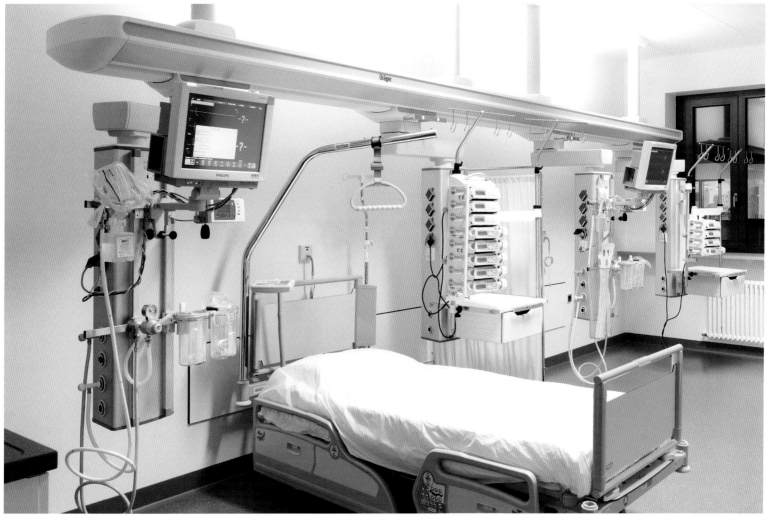

↑ | **Main view,** building volume
→ | **Glazed roof,** allowing daylight to flow inside

Queen Elizabeth Hospital

Birmingham

A dramatic addition to Birmingham's southern skyline, the new Queen Elizabeth Hospital is one of the largest in the United Kingdom and provides a 1,213-bed teaching hospital for the University Hospital Birmingham NHS (National Health Service) Foundation Trust. The project replaces two existing outdated hospitals, the adjacent Queen Elizabeth and neighboring Selly Oak Hospitals, bringing staff and treatment facilities together for greater efficiency. The 137,000-square-meter building houses an emergency department, 30 operating rooms, 15 specialist imaging suites, 15 laboratories, 300 teaching rooms and a 100-bed critical care department, the largest in Europe.

Address: Edgbaston, Birmingham B15 2TH, United Kingdom. **Client:** University Hospitals Birmingham NHS Foundation Trust. **Completion:** 2012. **Gross floor area:** 137,000 m². **Main materials:** unitized cladding panels, metal and glass finish. **Type:** general hospital. **Building:** new construction. **Treatment areas:** operating rooms, rehabilitation, physiotherapy. **Operator:** private and state.

←←| **Structural detail**
↑ | **View,** from access road
↙ | **Ground floor plan**

↑ | **DINZ,** connects the renovated existing building to the new building
→ | **Modern façade,** new building

Diagnostic-Internal-Neurological Center (DINZ)

Dresden

This Diagnostic-Internal-Neurological Center (DINZ) was built according to the competition-winning design from HWP Planungsgesellschaft and is the new focus of the Carl Gustav Carus University clinic at the TU Dresden, University of Technology. Comprising a new building and a renovated existing building with listed façade, DINZ is the result of an investment of 144 million Euros; the Free State of Saxony's biggest single investment in healthcare. The two building elements are connected by bridges and together house 419 beds and unite five clinics, as well as an institution that was previously divided between ten different buildings. Networking is the central architectural theme – characterized by its interaction with urban premises, by connections between the new and old, between interior and exterior, and by the relationship between humans and nature.

Address: Fetscherstraße 74, 01307 Dresden, Germany. **Client:** Free State of Saxony. **Completion:** 2012.
Gross floor area: 49,312 m². **Artists:** Judith Siegmund, Nikolaus Koliusis, Eva-Maria Wilde. **Main materi-als:** steel post and rail type façade, aluminum, wooden window frames. **Type:** general hospital. **Building:** new construction, renovation. **Treatment areas:** interdisciplinary emergency department, outpatient treat-ment areas, operating rooms. **Operator:** state. **Signage:** color coding specific to each floor.

↑ | Light-flooded entrance hall
← | Operating room

↑ | Nurses' station
↙ | Ground floor plan

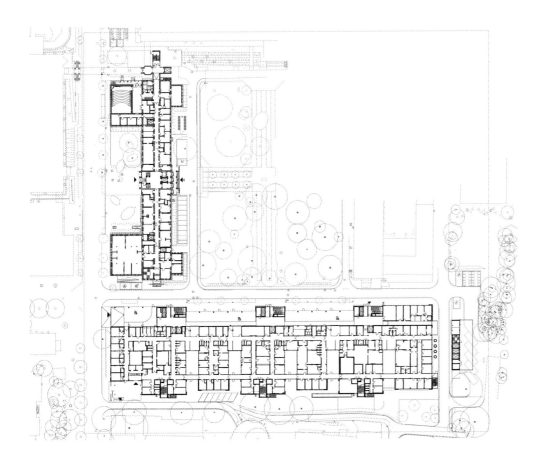

HSP
Hoppe Sommer
Planungsgesellschaft

↑ | **Entrance area**, with restaurant
↘ | **Sketch**, entrance hall

↗ | **General care and psychiatric ward**
→ | **Entrance hall**

District Clinics Esslingen

Kirchheim unter Teck

The plans and execution of the construction process for the Kirchheim clinic were completed as a part of the structural hospital reform in the district of Esslingen, Germany. Remodeling of the clinic was carried out in five construction phases. Through renovation of existing and addition of new buildings the hospital was comprehensively modernized. In the first phase the radiology and "LHKT" (left cardiac catheterdepartment) were modernized. The second phase involved the modernization of treatment building A, which houses examination and treatment areas. In the third phase the general care building B2 was added to complete the hospital structure. In the fourth phase the entrance hall and cafeteria / restaurant were redesigned. Finally in the fifth phase the psychiatric department through modernization of building D and new addition of building E will be accomplished in 2013. The hospital offers 301 beds.

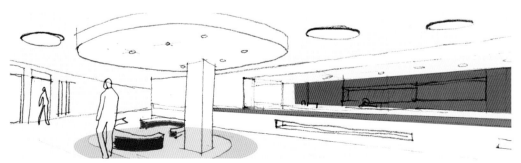

Address: Eugenstraße 3, 73230 Kirchheim unter Teck, Germany. **Client:** Landkreis Esslingen. **Completion:** 2012. **Gross floor area:** 36,358 m². **Main materials:** reinforced concrete, brick, aluminum façade. **Type:** general hospital, psychiatric care. **Building:** new construction, renovation. **Treatment areas:** operating rooms, rehabilitation, water therapy, physiotherapy. **Operator:** state.

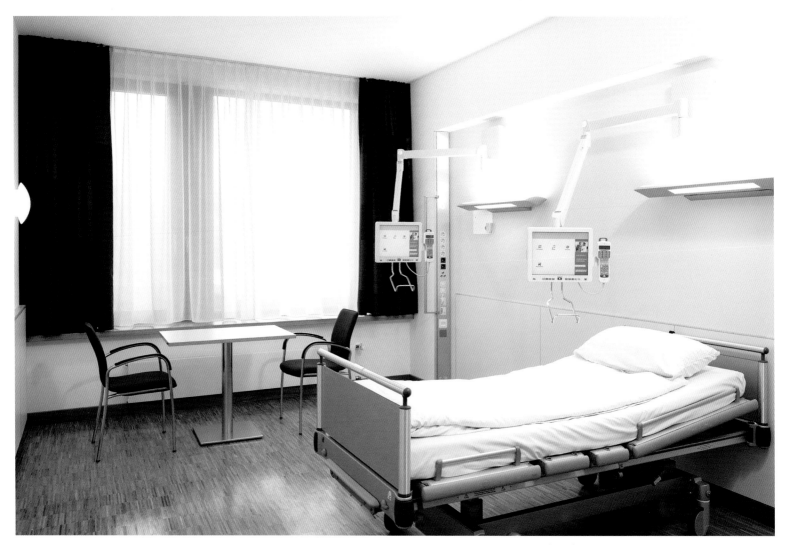

↑ | **Patient room**
↓ | **Sketch,** dining area

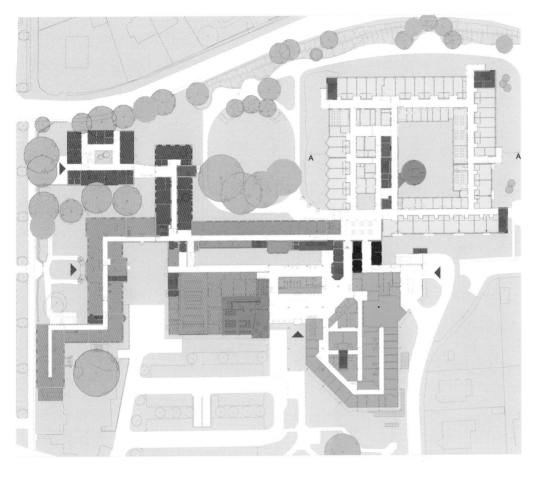

↖ | **Ground floor plan**
↓ | **Dining hall,** cafeteria

Sander Hofrichter
Architekten Partnerschaft

↑ | **View, from the Ihme**
↘ | **Section**

→ | **Entrance canopy**
↘ | **Entrance hall**

Clinic

Hanover

Located in Siloah, Hanover, the Siloah hospital and the Oststadt hospital have been combined into one new building. The new hospital has 529 beds, nine operating rooms, an interdisciplinary intensive care station with 60 beds, a cardiac catheter measuring facility, interdisciplinary endoscopy, pathology, laboratories, nuclear medicine, radiotherapy, physiotherapy and an interdisciplinary examination center, all of which adhere to the future-oriented design concept. The interior of the building is connected by a central access corridor, which leads to numerous waiting areas, coordinative offices and access routes to the upper floors. The upper floors accommodate the wards and are adapted to suit the individual needs of the different treatment functions.

Address: Ritter-Brüning-Straße/Stadionbrücke, 30449 Hanover, Germany. **Client:** Klinikum Region Hannover GmbH. **Completion:** 2014. **Gross floor area:** 64,641 m². **Main materials:** brick façade, glass curtain façade, reinforced concrete. **Type:** general hospital. **Building:** new construction. **Treatment areas:** operating rooms, physiotherapy. **Operator:** private. **Signage:** modern wayfinding system.

↑ | Two-bed patient room
↓ | Ground floor plan

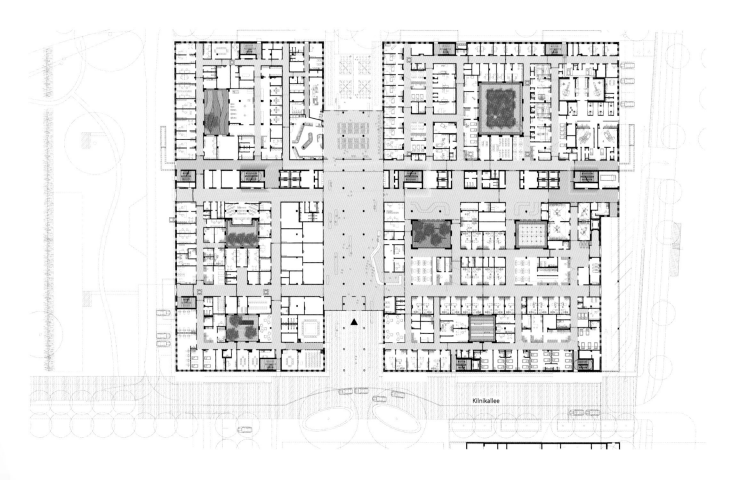

Kilnikallee

↑ | Courtyard
↙ | First floor plan

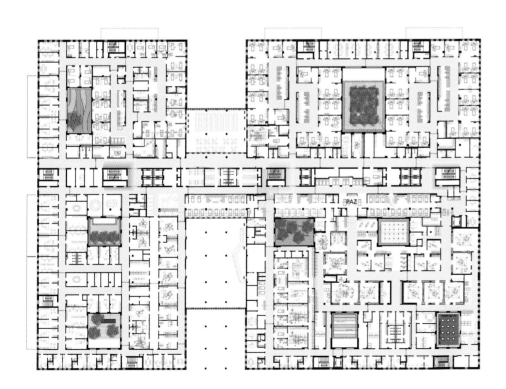

↑ | **Main view,** driveway
↗ | **Main entrance**
→ | **Reception**

Ravelo Medical Clinic

El Sauzal

This small clinic constitutes an abstract landmark in the rural environment, occupying an outstanding hillside position. The building has been designed on two levels with street-level pedestrian access: the main floor is occupied by the medical surgeries, while the lower floor houses multipurpose and staff areas. The project is characterized by a dialogue between the continuous internal wooden cladding, which separates the areas for specific medical uses from the public ones, and the external concrete frame, which lends the building its urban presence. The panoramic window embraces the distant countryside, incorporating it into the everyday life of the clinic, converting the waiting area into a room with scenic views, a therapeutic space.

PROJECT FACTS

Address: Calle Hoya de la Viuda s/n, Ravelo, 38359 El Sauzal, Spain. **Client:** Canary Islands Government: Health and Consume Council. **Completion:** 2007. **Gross floor area:** 706 m². **Main materials:** concrete, glass, plywood, aluminum. **Type:** general, pediatrics. **Building:** new construction. **Treatment areas:** physiotherapy. **Operator:** state.

↑ | **Waiting area**
↙ | **Street elevation**

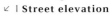

↑ | Exterior view
↓ | First floor plan

Casa Sólo Arquitectos

↑ | Exterior boulevard view
↗ | General exterior view
→ | Covered leisure area

Santa Lucía General University Hospital

Cartagena

This hospital has a textile architectural envelope, shaped to complement the hilly surrounding landscape. The faceted screen cuts the building height to a more human scale and provides solar protection to the southern façades. Its colors change with daylight at different times of the day to achieve the total integration of such a big structure within the environment. The program's objective is to encourage a stronger integration of the community into the hospital area. The general access concourse is an unheated structure that provides a transition between exterior and interior and also houses the leisure facilities.

PROJECT FACTS

Address: Cale Mezquita, s/n, Paraje Los Arcos, 30202, Cartagena, Spain. **Client:** Giscarmsa Sau. **Completion:** 2010. **Gross floor area:** 114,369 m². **Main materials:** stretched plastic mesh, aluminum, natural stone, PVC. **Type:** general hospital. **Building:** new construction. **Treatment areas:** operating rooms, rehabilitation, water therapy, physiotherapy. **Operator:** state. **Signage:** room numbers integrated into flooring and walls.

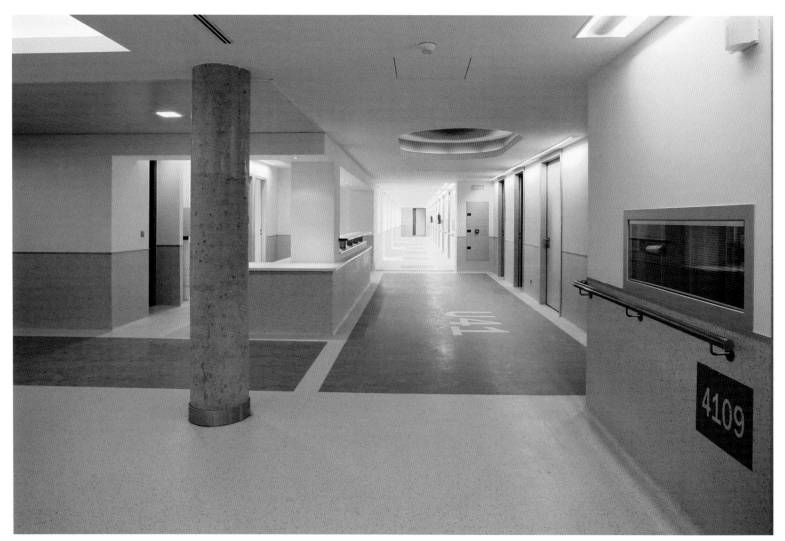

↑ | **Inpatient area,** room numbers integrated into PVC
↓ | **Ground floor plan**

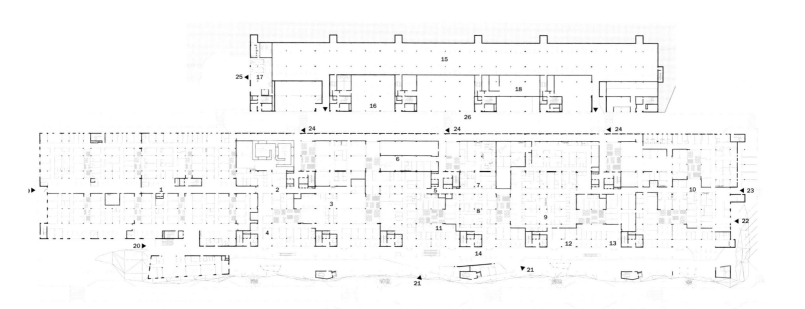

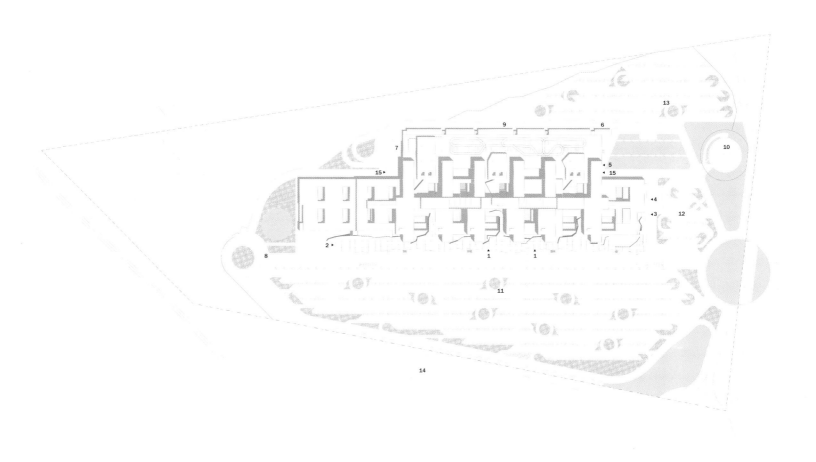

↑ | Site plan
↓ | Running track and sports area

| Jean Philippe Pargade

↑ | **Façade**
↘ | **Building volume**

Sarthe-et-Loir Health Center

Le Bailleul

The new Sarthe-et-Loir Health Center was built as a hilltop beacon in the middle of farmland. A tension is created between the rural landscape and the technological elegance of the building. The horizontal architecture of this hospital environment is one of the first constructions of its type to be organized as a networked system. Extensive continuous floor levels pierced by large and small patios and served by a central artery provide a high level of operational flexibility. The sensitive façade of silk-screen-printed glass is animated by the musical rhythm of the windows. The color treatment of the interior spaces plays a major role and reveals the vital contribution to the clinics that has been made by the use of artwork.

Address: La chasse du point du jour, BP 10129 Le Beilleul, France. **Client:** Pôle Santé Sarthe-et-Loir. **Completion:** 2007. **Gross floor area:** 34,000 m². **Landscape architects:** David Besson Girard. **Color specialist:** Gary Glaser. **Main materials:** concrete, screenprinted glass. **Type:** general hospital. **Building:** new construction. **Treatment areas:** operating rooms. **Operator:** state.

↑ | **Patio**

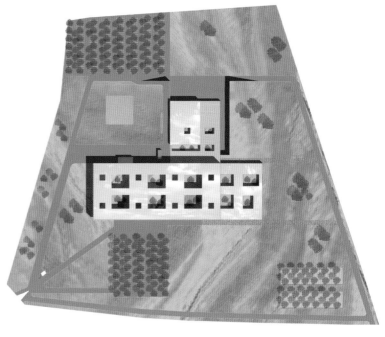

↑ | **Master plan**
↓ | **Hospital,** in countryside setting

C. F. Møller Architects

↑ | **View of western façade,** treatment buildings and emergencies intake
→ | **Wood and natural stone,** dominate glazed, internal street

Akershus University Hospital

Lørenskog

This new university hospital is not a traditional institution building; it is a friendly, informal place with open and comprehensible surroundings oriented toward the patients and their relatives. The hospital's various departments all differ in their dimensions, form and expression. The wards have one kind of architectural expression, the treatment departments have another, and the children's clinic has an expression all of its own. This helps to create a varied visual experience, while at the same time making it easy to find your way around. The design of the complex reveals the influence of the high priority given to daylight for all workplaces, views of the surrounding landscape, and contact with the outside environment.

PROJECT FACTS

Address: Sykehusveien 27, 1478 Lørenskog, Norway. **Client:** Helse SØR-ØST-RHF. **Completion:** 2012.
Gross floor area: 118,000 m². **Landscape architects:** Bjørbekk & Lindheim AS, Schønherr Landskab
A/S. **Main materials:** brick screens, rendered façades. **Type:** general hospital. **Building:** new construction. **Staff areas:** staff rooms, lockers, canteen, fitness room. **Treatment areas:** operating rooms, water
therapy, physiotherapy. **Operator:** state.

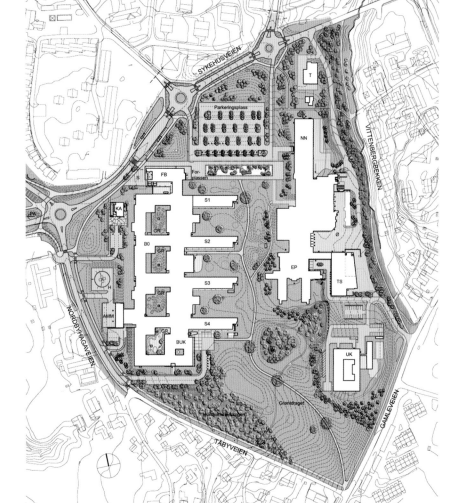

↑ | **Exterior view,** complex and front building
← | **Site plan**

← | **Detail of the balconies,** lighting and materials of the glazed street
↓ | **Canteen,** enriched with art work

Dietmar Feichtinger Architectes
Priebernig. 'P'
Müller & Klinger Architects Collective
FCP Fritsch, Chiari & Partner

↑ | **Canopy**, entrance
↗ | **Foyer**
→ | **Waiting area**

Clinic

Klagenfurt

The design for the district hospital LKH Klagenfurt was chosen as the winner of a two-stage design competition and is innovative in many ways. The latest medical technology, combined with an enhanced cross-utilization of medical equipment and facilities, give this new hospital a pioneering status in Europe. The footprint of the building is largely determined by landscaped courtyards which open it up to the site. The flat low-lying structure merges easily with the low and heterogeneous urban surroundings of Klagenfurt. The comb-like organization of the buildings provides a strong visual relationship to the surrounding green areas for both the accommodation and medical wards. Thus, the hospital rooms, access halls and waiting areas all become sun-drenched and comfortable health-stimulating light therapy rooms. This tangible connection to the natural surrounds is an integral part of the new hospital Klagenfurt.

Address: St. Veiter Straße 4, 9020 Klagenfurt, Austria. **Client:** LKH Klagenfurt. **Completion:** 2010.
Gross floor area: 145,000 m². **Main materials:** metal, glass. **Type:** general hospital. **Building:** new construction. **Treatment areas:** operating room. **Operator:** state.

↑ | **Aerial view**
← | **Intensive care unit**

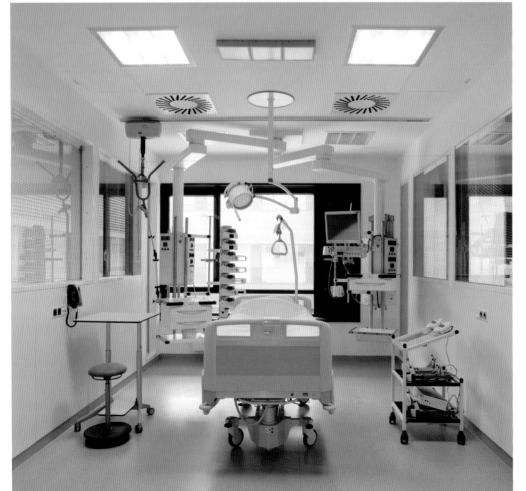

↑ | North link
↙ | First floor plan

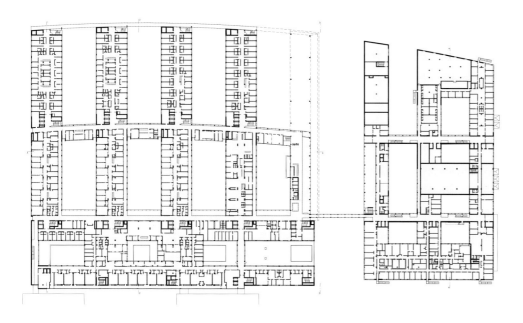

Brullet Pineda Arquitectos

↑ | **Building volumes,** determined by site terrain
↗ | **Exterior**
→ | **Daylit seating area**

Doctor Moisès Broggi Hospital

Sant Joan Despí

The Sant Joan Despí Doctor Moisès Broggi Hospital is a new construction that caters for a population of 300,000 people. The organization of the hospital is determined by the access and the topographic conditions of the land. The main access is located along the southeast of the plot, at the highest point. The healthcare and public corridors do not interact with each other and an independent entrance for outpatient services allows the access to external visitors from two different entrances. Sustainability was an important part of the design process from the beginning. Energy efficiency has been obtained thanks to the building's orientation, closed toward the north and open towards the south, and the façade design with brise-soleils that controls the natural sunlight. Photovoltaic installations and rainwater re-use systems were also added.

Address: Calle Jacint Verdaguer 90, 08970 – Sant Joan Despí, Barcelona, Spain. **Client:** Consorci Sanitari Integral. **Co-architects:** Alfonso de Luna, Marcial Novo. **Completion:** 2010. **Gross floor area:** 43,360 m². **Main materials:** red cedar, glass, curved aluminum panels. **Type:** general hospital. **Building:** new construction. **Treatment areas:** operating rooms, rehabilitation, physiotherapy. **Operator:** state.

↑ | **Entrance**
↓ | **Sections**

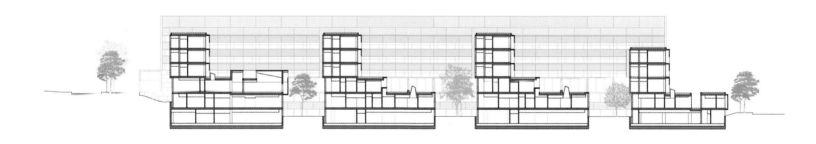

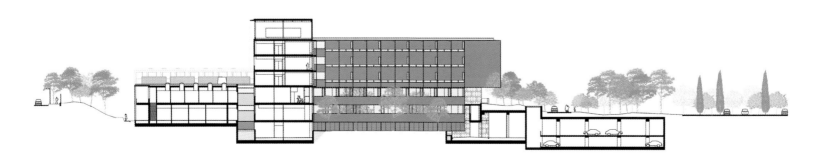

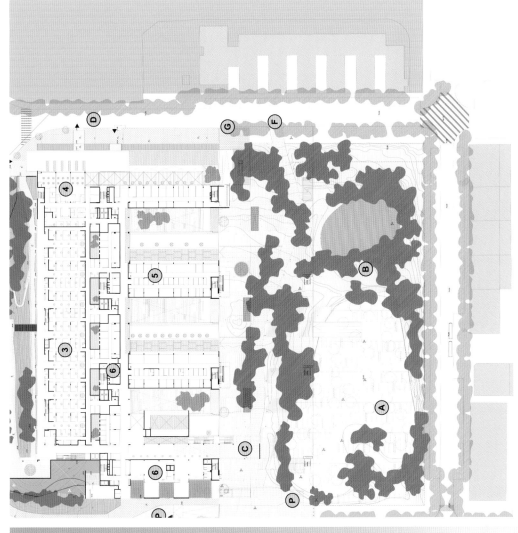

↖ | Site plan
↓ | Foyer

↑ | **Main view,** at night
↗ | **Hallway,** with glazed roof
→ | **Waiting area**

Broomfield Hospital

Chelmsford

Llewelyn Davies Yeang was the architect and design team leader for this development and also provided interior design, landscape design lend statutory planning services. The development brief sets out to centralize and modernize acute services provided by the Mid Essex Hospital National Health Service Trust, integrating the new facility with retained estate. The new accommodation provides a major accident and emergency unit with 110 assessment beds, maternity department, expanded outpatients department, new imaging facilities and an elective care center with five operating theatres and three endoscopy suites. Altogether there are 361 new beds and neo-natal places in a 50,000-square-meter new build project plus a new decked car park with 457 spaces.

Address: Court Road, Chelmsford, CM1 7ET, United Kingdom. **Client:** Mid Essex Hospital Services NHS Trust. **Completion:** 2010. **Gross floor area:** 50,000 m². **Type:** general hospital. **Building:** new construction. **Treatment areas:** operating theater, rehabilitation. **Operator:** state.

↑ | **Main entrance**
↓ | **Plan**, promenade

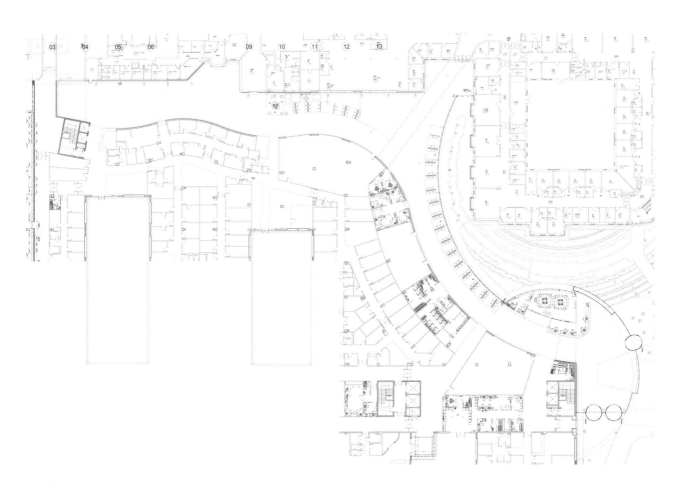

↑ | **Lobby**
↙ | **Sketch,** patient room

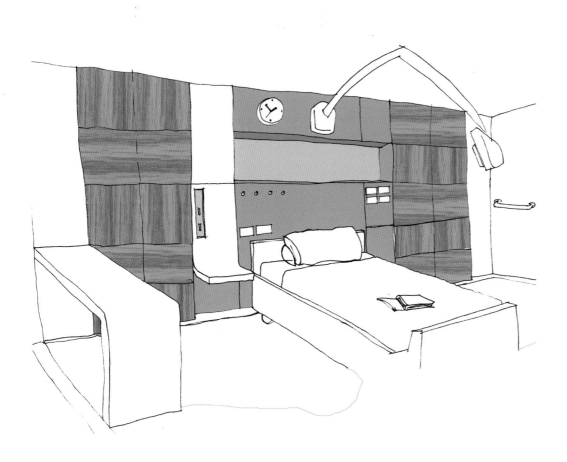

↑ | **Main view**
↓ | **Section,** courtyards and main access

Hospital

Molde

The architectural goals of Molde Hospital are ambitious and multifaceted. Efficiency and flexibility are programmatic desires that must be balanced with the emotional needs of the patients. The architects believe it is important to reduce the alienating experience of the "treatment machine". The hospital is divided into horizontally layered zones. Treatment areas, technical services, outpatient care and surgical areas are housed within a low-base structure. Patient room areas are placed high in the building structure to give all rooms views to the fjord. These elements together with roof gardens and inner courtyards play an important role in creating a sense of well-being and connectivity to the outside world.

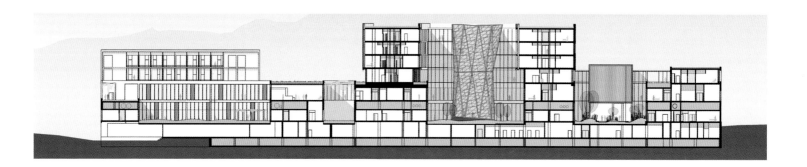

Address: 6400 Molde, Norway. **Client:** Helsebygg Midtnorge and Helse Møre og Romsdal HF. **Completion:** 2018. **Gross floor area:** 45,000 m². **Planning partners:** Arkitema Architects. **Main materials:** concrete, brick, wood. **Type:** general hospital. **Building:** new construction. **Treatment areas:** operating rooms, rehabilitation, physiotherapy. **Operator:** state.

↑ | **Bird's-eye view**
↓ | **Traffic chart**

↓ | **Façade**

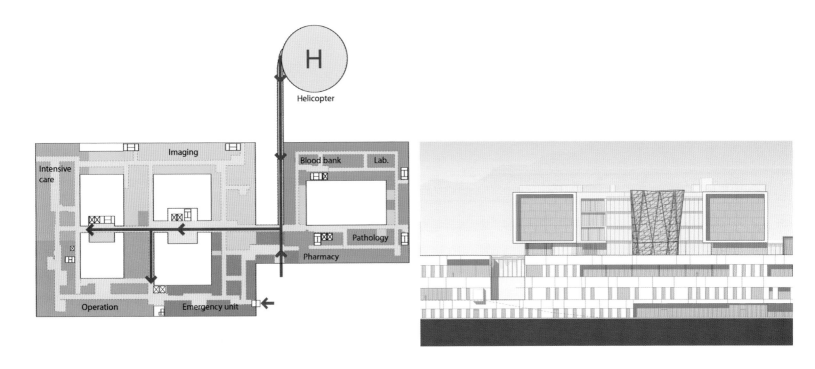

MVentura & Partners

↑ | **Eastern façade,** at dusk
↗ | **Main view,** reflecting sunset
→ | **Lobby,** waiting area on gallery and staircase

Hospital CUF

Porto

This hospital of the Companhia União Fabril comprises two overlapping volumetric structures. The upper volume is clad with glass and steel and cantilevers eight meters over the more opaque volume below. The upper volume houses the patient wards, while the more technical areas including triage assessment areas and operating rooms, are located in the basement. The modular structure organizes all segments of the complex program and is visible in the outward expression of the elevations as well as in the design of the large foyer which is opened out by a large atrium.

PROJECT FACTS

Address: Estrada da Circunvalação, 14341 Porto, Portugal. **Client:** José de Mello Saúde. **Completion:** 2010. **Gross floor area:** 44,000 m². **Main materials:** concrete, glass, aluminum. **Type:** general hospital. **Building:** new construction. **Staff areas:** restaurant, cafeteria, auditorium. **Treatment areas:** operating rooms, physiotherapy. **Operator:** private.

↑ | **Corridor,** surgery unit
↙ | **Ground floor plan**

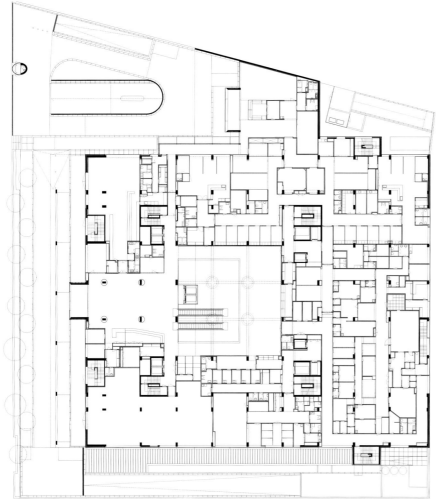

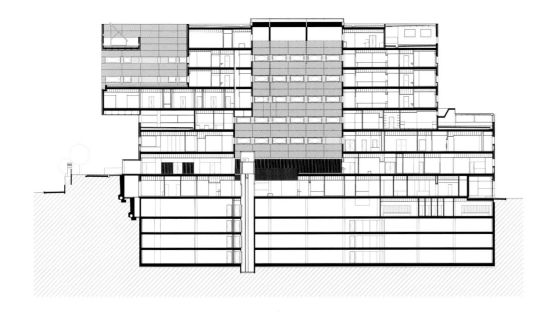

↖ | **Cross section**
↓ | **Detail,** skylight view

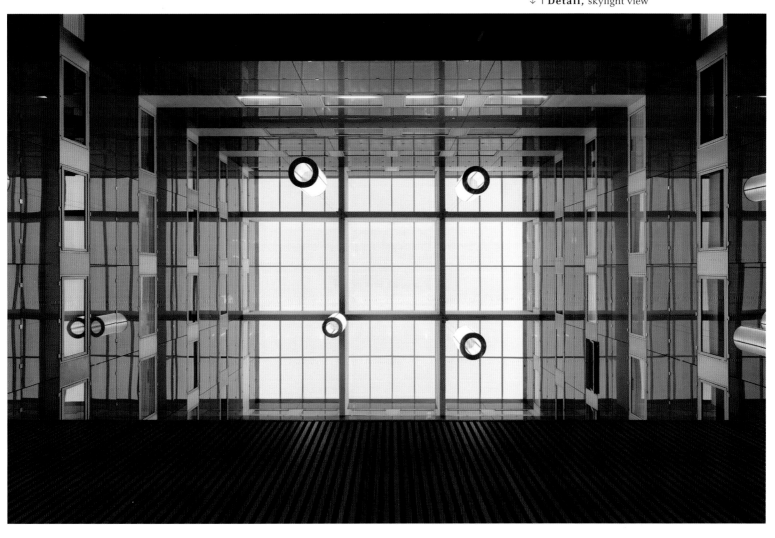

TASH –
Taller de Arquitectura

↑ | Main entrance
↓ | Sections

University General Hospital

Toledo

The design of this contemporary hospital was conceived through analysis of recent hospital architecture and proposes a high flexibility for adaptation to technologic change and medical advance, as well as offering the best medical care. A central street is the main structure connecting the various functions. Consultations and examination rooms configure a linear diagnosis block, located at the center of the complex. The inpatient areas and specialized units are accessible from the main street. A volumetric gradation from the central core of the building to the lower exterior parts gives the large structure a more human scale.

Address: C/ La Granada 2, 45001 Toledo, Spain. **Client:** SESCAM. **Completion:** ongoing. **Gross floor area:** 320,000 m². **Main materials:** concrete, pre-cast concrete blocks, steel, glass. **Type:** general hospital. **Building:** new construction. **Treatment areas:** operating rooms, rehabilitation, water therapy, physiotherapy. **Operator:** state.

↑ | **Central street**

↑ | **Lobby**
↓ | **Ground floor plan**

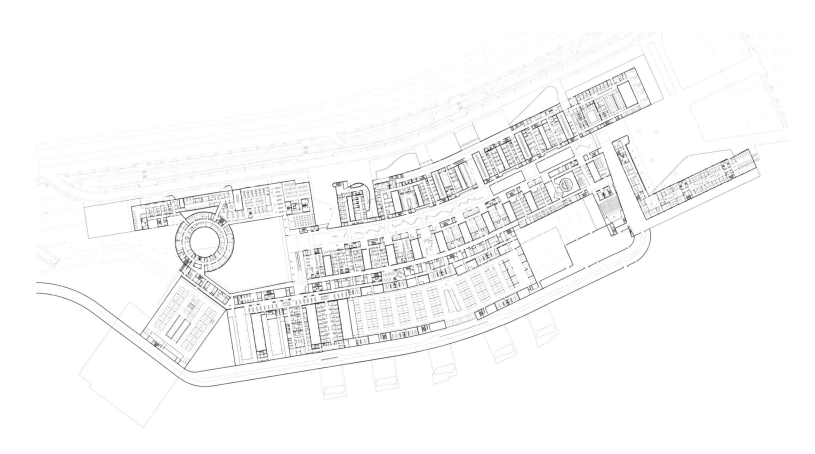

↑ | Corridor
↓ | Main view

Aurora

Odense

The new Odense University Hospital (OUH) embodies an innovative building of high architectural quality, designed to meet the requirements and challenges of tomorrow. Like its namesake the goddess Aurora, the hospital finds renewal in the transition between old and new – and the conversion from tradition to modernity. The human scale supports the conception of the hospital as the good host and a place where patients and visitors can easily orient themselves and feel at home. The New OUH and the Faculty of Health Sciences are situated in a special location in Odense – close to the city center but, at the same time, within a scenic landscape of dense old forests, extensive fields, hedges, ponds and waterways.

Address: Sdr. Boulevard 29, 5000 Odense C, Denmark. **Client:** The Region of Southern Denmark and the Danish University and Property Agency. **Completion:** design 2011. **Gross floor area:** 234,000 m². **Planning partners:** Friis & Moltke, Arkitektfirmaet TKT. **Landscaping architects:** SLA. **Main materials:** concrete, glass, wood. **Type:** general hospital. **Building:** new construction.

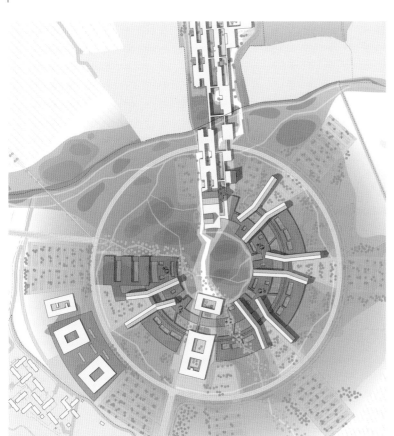

↑ | Site plan

↑ | Bird's-eye view
↓ | Foyer

↑ | **General hospital,** entrance to acute and general medicine
↗ | **Main entrance,** view of the central green
→ | **Foyer,** entrance hall and waiting area

Krankenhaus Hedwigshöhe
Hospital and Psychiatric Units

Berlin

In terms of urban development, Hedwigshöhe hospital completes the garden city of Falkenberg on the outskirts of Berlin. The existing bell tower is visible from afar and highlights the new village green, which is framed and completed by various buildings. The original villa and tower remain as freestanding buildings. New additions to the ensemble include staggered pavilions for the psychiatric department and a horizontal structure housing acute general medicine, completed in 2008. The architects' deliberate intention was to create a small hospital town that architecturally shares a dialogue with both the historical original buildings and the modern new additions.

Address: Höhensteig 1, 12526 Berlin, Germany. **Client:** St. Hedwig Kliniken Berlin GmbH represented by Agamus Dienstleistungs-GmbH. **Completion:** 2008. **Gross floor area:** 23,300 m². **Planning partners:** M. Brullet, A. de Pineda, Barcelona. **Main materials:** wood, plaster. **Type:** general, psychiatric. **Building:** new construction, renovation. **Staff areas:** staff room with kitchen. **Treatment areas:** operating rooms, intensive care, rehabilitation, physiotherapy, psychotherapy, psychiatry. **Operator:** nonprofit.

↑ | **West façade,** bell tower in background
← | **Interior courtyard**

← | **Perspective**, horizontal wooden cladding
↓ | **First floor plan**

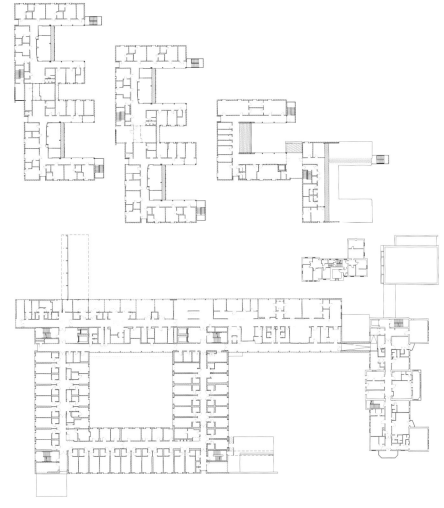

↑ | **Main view,** entrance general hospital
↗ | **Bird's-eye view,** site
→ | **Terrace,** cafeteria

Sheikh Khalifa Medical City

Abu Dhabi

Conceived as three hospitals under one roof, the new Sheikh Khalifa Medical City (SKMC) is a 278,700-square-meter, 850-bed medical complex combining a general hospital, with a level one trauma center, and tertiary women's and pediatric hospitals. Envisioned as a city within a city, the design defies the typical model of a medical center and creates a bustling campus-like environment of distinct character, vibrant public spaces and a sense of community. The hospitality-inspired facility offers a lively town center of cafes, retail, prayer rooms and education spaces, as well as a shaded rooftop oasis. The three hospitals are each uniquely branded but maintain an overall unified expression. SKMC will be the largest hospital in the UAE and the first to achieve an Estidama sustainability rating.

Address: Abu Dhabi, UAE. **Client:** SEHA, Abu Dhabi Health Services Co. **Completion:** 2016. **Gross floor area:** 278,700 m². **Planning partners:** IMCE, Tilke. **Main materials:** stone, glass, powder-coated metal sun screens. **Type:** emergency medicine, neo-natal, pediatrics, obstetrics, general. **Building:** new construction. **Treatment areas:** operating rooms, rehabilitation. **Operator:** state.

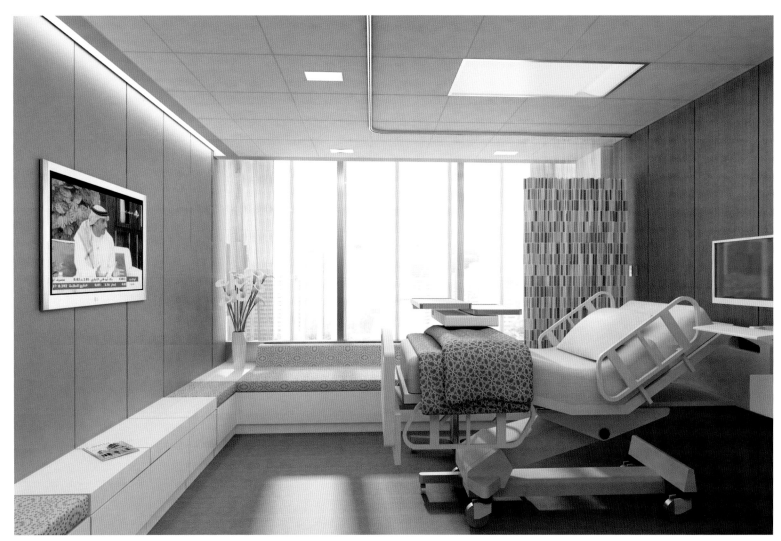

↑ | **Patient room,** general hospital
← | **Typical bed floor plan**

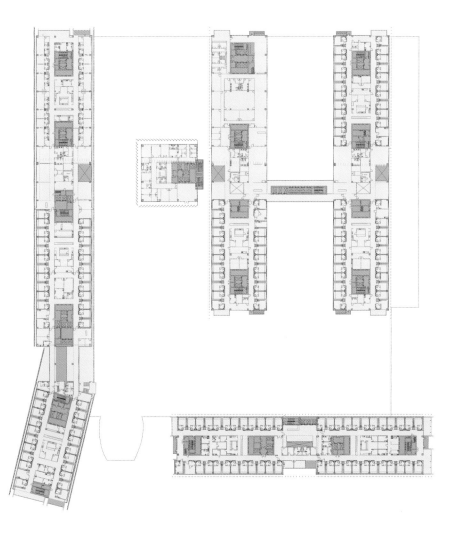

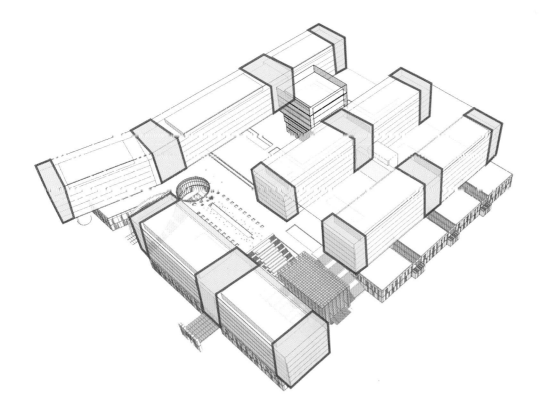

↖ | **Diagram,** green space in bed towers
↓ | **Fabric membrane roof**

Henning Larsen Architects

↑ | **Main view,** from street
↓ | **Section**
↘↘ | **Sketch**

University Hospital

Copenhagen

Copenhagen University Hospital, known nationally as Rigshospitalet, is located in a dense urban context in the city capital and is Denmark's premiere hospital housing the country's most complex clinical specializations. The original 1970s building has 1,120 beds and serves 65,000 inpatients and approximately 420,000 outpatients annually. In addition to 8,000 personnel, the hospital trains and hosts medical and other healthcare science students and scientists. The hospital requires an extensive addition to double its operational capacity. The extension includes a new otolaryngology department, parking structure, and hospital hotel to accommodate out-of-town relatives that want to be close to patients during their treatment and recovery.

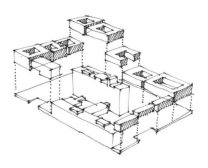

Address: Blegdamsvej 9, 2100 Copenhagen, Denmark. **Client:** Region Hovedstaden/RKB Rigshospitalets Kvalitetsfonds Byggeprojekt. **Completion:** design 2011. **Gross floor area:** 76,900 m². **Planning partners:** Brunsgaard & Laursen, Lohfert & Lohfert, Friis og Moltke. **Main materials:** brick, glass, steel. **Type:** general hospital. **Building:** new construction. **Operator:** state.

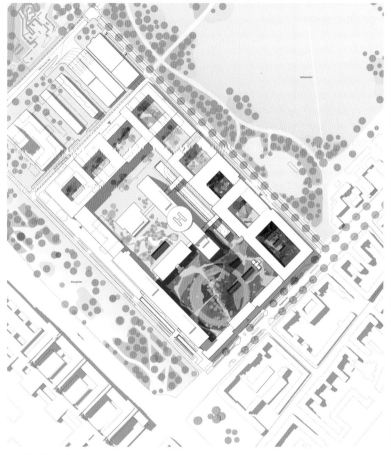

↑ | Site plan

↑ | Courtyard
↓ | Lobby, auditorium

↑ | **General view**, at night
↗ | **Main façade**
→ | **Entrance hall**

Los Arcos del Mar Menor University Hospital

San Javier

The main façade, looking south, has two of the building's main innovations: a brise-soleil protecting the administration departments, designed with transparent photovoltaic cell panels, and a 120-meter long LED information panel – currently the longest in Europe – which penetrates into the main hall. The open scheme on the north-west side allows the addition of a series of new modules. Good exposure to natural light is a factor of great importance in this type of building, and the design thus incorporates a system of generously sized patios, fully incorporated into the structural grid, to provide the different departments with fresh air and sunlight.

PROJECT FACTS

Address: Paraje Torre Octavio, 54, 30739 San Javier, Spain. **Client:** Giscarmsa Sau. **Completion:** 2010. **Gross floor area:** 61,352 m². **Main materials:** porcelain stoneware tiles, aluminum, PVC. **Type:** general hospital. **Building:** new construction. **Treatment areas:** operating rooms, rehabilitation, water therapy, physiotherapy. **Operator:** state. **Signage:** room numbers integrated into walls and floors.

↑ | Inpatient control unit
↓ | Sections

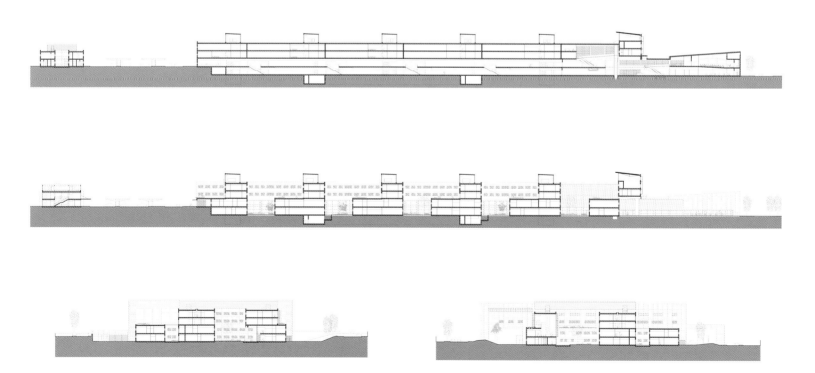

↑ | **Detail**, courtyard façade
↓ | **First floor plan**

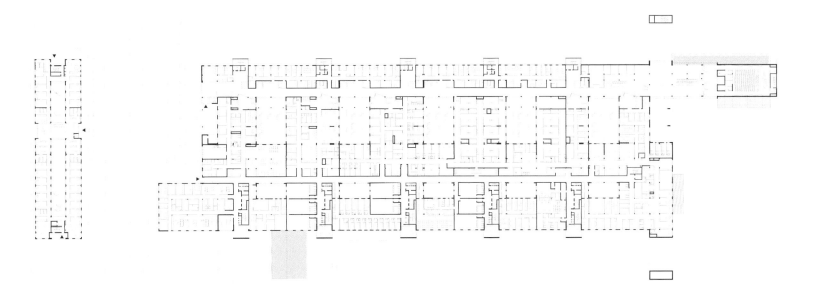

↑ | **Waiting area**, with green couches
→ | **Courtyard,** at dusk

Private Hospital

Guimarães

Guimarães Private Hospital is located outside of thé urban perimeter, near a set of recently developed facilities by the Guimarães City Council. The site criteria conditioned the building size and its distribution into two clearly perceptible units. The building elements form a patio and are united by vertical and horizontal circulation components to which public horizontal circulation areas correspond schematically with direct natural lighting, and internal circulation areas for services, or mixed use, mainly artificially lit, which will allow the easy identification of the type of circulation by this simple coding throughout the whole building. The compact size and clear organization contributes to that objective.

PROJECT FACTS

133

Address: Santiago de Candoso, 4835-235 Guimarães, Portugal. **Client:** Edisamus Ivestimentos Imobiliáries na Saúde. **Completion:** 2009. **Gross floor area:** 14,087 m². **Planning partners:** Fernando Torres, Marlene Sousa, Francisco Oliveira, Helio Pinto, Joao Carvalho. **Main materials:** aluminum, laminated glass, iron, mosaic sandstone. **Type:** general hospital. **Building:** new construction. **Operator:** private.

← | **Glass bridge,** connecting buildings
↓ | **First floor plan**

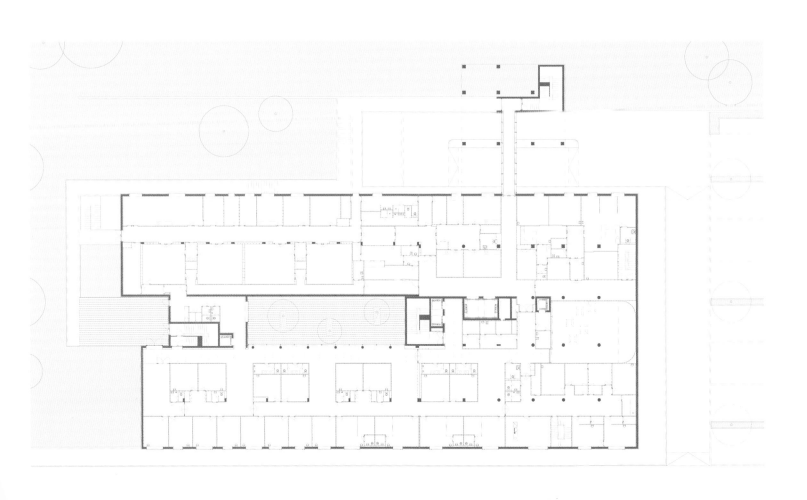

↑ | **Hall,** waiting area and staircase
↙ | **Sections**

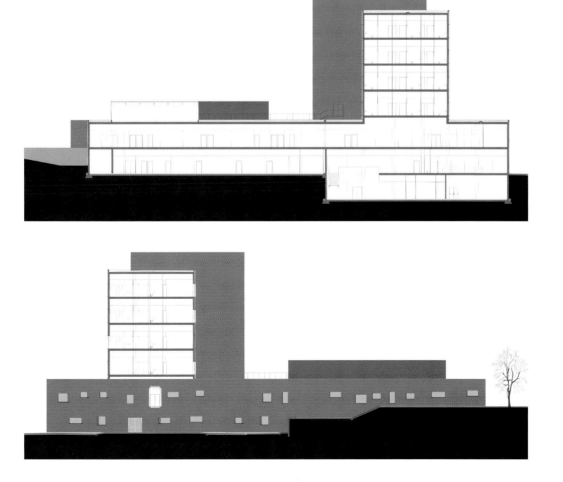

↑ | **Bellevue Hospital exterior,** looking north on First Avenue
→ | **Atrium,** with existing building on left

Bellevue Hospital Center Ambulatory Care Facility

New York City

The new Ambulatory Care Facility, together with renovated medical spaces within the existing Bellevue Hospital complex, has radically transformed a venerable New York City institution into an advanced medical campus. In addition to accommodating an essential medical function, the new building serves as the main entrance for the entire hospital complex, reintroducing the architecture of the historic McKim, Mead & White buildings to thousands of daily visitors. The primary design challenge was to transform the close physical proximity of the existing and new buildings into a spatial and symbolic generosity. By bringing together old and new, the glazed atrium has become the emblematic heart of Bellevue Hospital.

PROJECT FACTS

Address: 462 First Avenue, New York City, NY 10016, USA. **Client:** Dormitory Authority of the State of New York. **Completion:** 2005. **Gross floor area:** 19,510 m² (new building), 12,821 m² (renovation). **Renovation architects:** Guenther 5 Architects. **Main materials:** aluminum and glass curtain wall, brick masonry, granite floor and masonry walls in atrium. **Type:** general hospital. **Building:** new construction, renovation. **Treatment areas:** operating rooms. **Operator:** state.

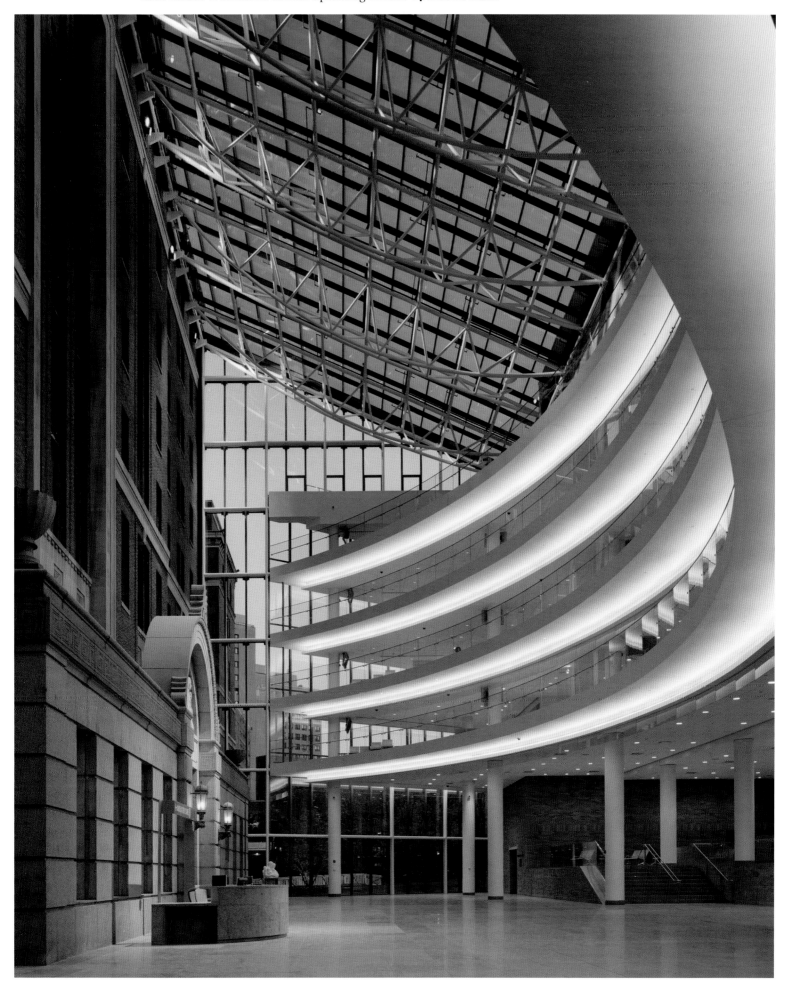

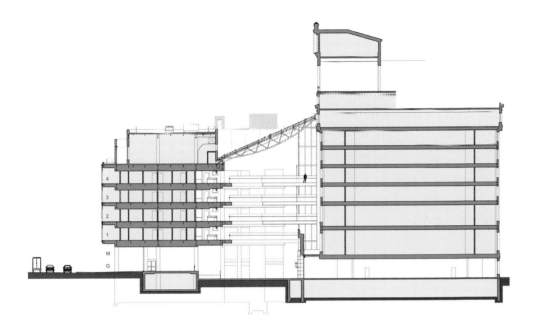

←←| **Atrium detail,** with façade of existing building
↑ | **Section**
↓ | **Patient waiting area,** overlooking the atrium

↑ | **Building volume,** wood bent into form while still green and flexible
→ | **Light-filled waiting area**

Pictou Landing Health Center

Nova Scotia

The building design for the Pictou Landing Health Center is based on a strategy of maximizing the use of local materials and skills. The structural system was developed through a study of traditional Mi'kmaq long house and lodge construction, using locally available wood in the round, bent into arched forms while green and flexible, to maximize their structural efficiency and minimize the embodied energy inputs. The heating, cooling and air exchange systems minimize the environmental impacts of the building over time by using ground source heat and cooling. The height and slope of the cross section allows for the efficient capture of return air and heat recovery ventilation. The lower level is bermed into the sloped earth, and the thermal mass of the building at the lower level enhances energy efficiency.

Address: 14 Maple Street, B0K 1X0 Nova Scotia, Canada. **Client:** Pictou Landing Mi'kmaq First Nation Health Canada. **Completion:** 2008. **Gross floor area:** 1,200 m². **Main materials:** local timber. **Type:** general hospital. **Building:** new construction. **Operator:** state.

↑ | **Interior,** lower level
↙ | **Design sketch**

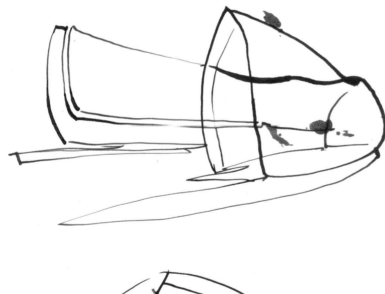

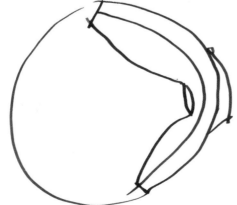

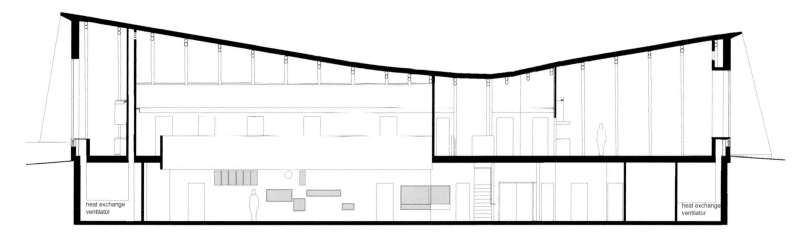

heat exchange ventilator

heat exchange ventilator

↑ | **Longitudinal section**
↓ | **Volume,** reflecting traditional architectural forms

INTERDISCIPLINARY

↑ | **View**, from south-east
→ | **Detail**, façade

University Clinic Pediatrics and Cardiology

Innsbruck

This new pediatrics and cardiology center fits seamlessly into the intact urban fabric of the city. The aim of the design was to create bright, daylit interior rooms and corridors that would transform the time of day and the seasons into a tangible experience, and to offer patients, visitors and personnel high-quality facilities. Despite the stringent spatial program, additional generously sized individual areas were created for patients and caregivers. The most important connective element in the new building is the access corridor, a main circulation route that connects the clinic's entire first and second floors. This access corridor is the building's main "artery" and includes recreation areas, play zones, drawing corners and quiet zones, all of which offer views of the imposing surrounding mountains.

PROJECT FACTS

Address: Anichstraße 35, 6020 Innsbruck, Austria. **Client:** TILAK – Tiroler Landeskrankenanstalten GmbH. **Completion:** 2008. **Gross floor area:** 17,400 m². **Structural engineers:** CBP Cronauer Beratung Planung, Munich. **Landscape architects:** UGC Planungsgruppe Landschaftsarchitekten, Munich. **Main materials:** aluminum, glass, reinforced concrete. **Type:** pediatrics, cardiology. **Building:** new construction. **Treatment areas:** operating rooms. **Operator:** state.

↑ | **Nurses' station,** fourth floor
↓ | **Ground floor plan**

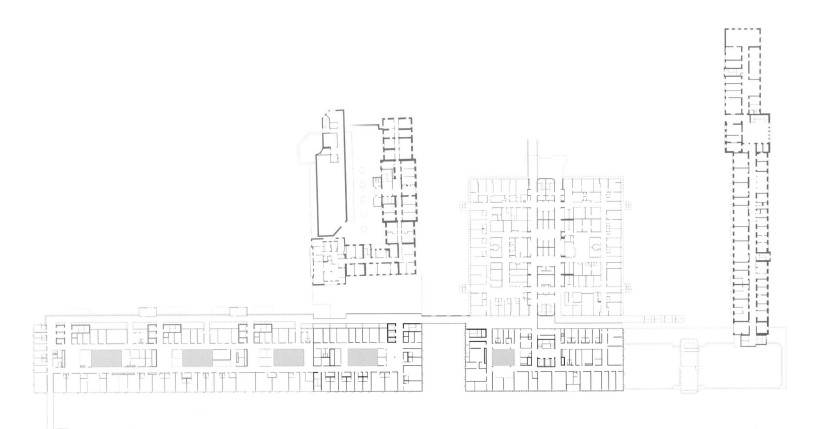

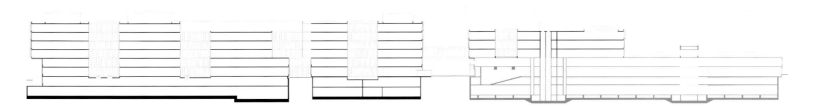

↑ | **Section**
↓ | **Main entrance,** to the east of building

The Manser Practice
Architects & Designers

↑ | **New ward block,** next to original
→ | **Colored glass detail**

Acute Ward Block

Chesterfield

This new building provides three vertically stacked 32-bed wards to supplement the 550 beds that were at full capacity. It provides state-of-the-art ward facilities where patient care and dignity, infection control and a healing environment were key elements of the brief. The T-shaped plan reinvents the traditional ward layout to improve staff efficiency and patient dignity. By designing each ward in two clusters of patient rooms, each around a nurse base, with a shared support hub. A new link bridge directly connects the new accommodation to the existing hospital streets, incorporating full-height artist-designed colored glass louvres that protect the privacy of patients in the adjacent existing ward rooms.

PROJECT FACTS

Address: Chesterfield Road, Calow, Chesterfield S44 5BL, United Kingdom. **Client:** Chesterfield Royal Hospital NHS Foundation Trust. **Completion:** 2010. **Gross floor area:** 4,055 m². **Main materials:** ceramic granite, colored glass. **Type:** acute wards. **Building:** new construction. **Treatment areas:** isolation rooms, quiet rooms, treatment rooms. **Operator:** state. **Signage:** custom-designed by The Manser Practice.

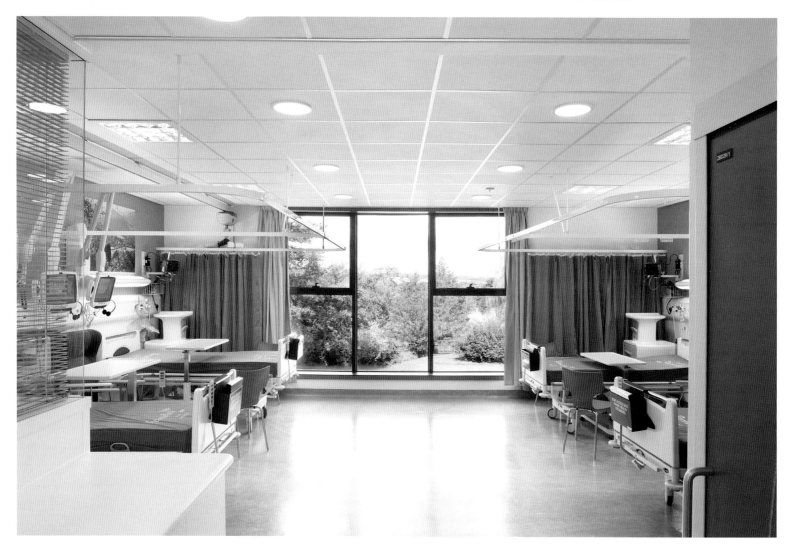

↑ | Four-bed ward
↙ | Typical floor plan

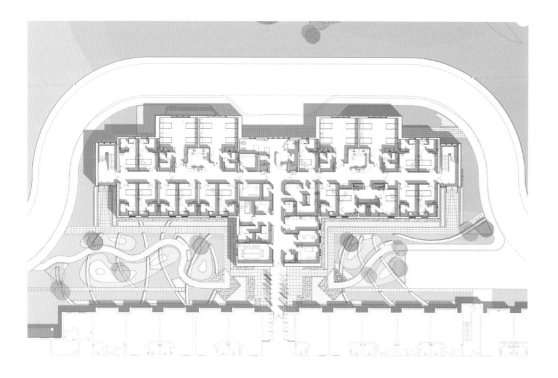

↑ | **New ward,** at dusk
↙ | **Site plan**

↑ | **Detail**, façade
→ | **Conference room**

Children's Hematology, Oncology and Immunology Clinic

Moscow

The architecture of the Federal Scientific Clinical Center of Pediatric Hematology, Oncology and Immunology, named after Dmitry Rogachev, is designed for and inspired by children. Illuminated colors and expressive architectural language characterize the outside as well as the inside, creating a welcoming atmosphere that helps to reduce patient anxiety. The dynamic structure with its vibrant ambience is conducive to fast healing and recuperation and also created a pleasant and supportive working environment for hospital personnel. The building's structure is defined by spatially and functionally separated blocks. Each block with its respective function is allocated a colorful theme; an arrangement that also serves to aid orientation.

Address: Samory Maschela Street, 117198 Moscow, Russia. **Client:** Federal Scientific Clinical Center of Pediatric Hematology, Oncology and Immunology named after Dmitry Rogachev. **Completion:** 2011. **Gross floor area:** 72,000 m². **Design and planning approval:** Alexander Asadov, Studio Asadov. **Interior Design:** Bettina Koenen. **Design and implementation planning:** Torsten Meyer, Hospital Technology. **Main materials:** façade cladding, aluminum. **Type:** pediatrics, cancer. **Building:** new construction. **Operator:** state.

↑ | Playroom
← | Operating room

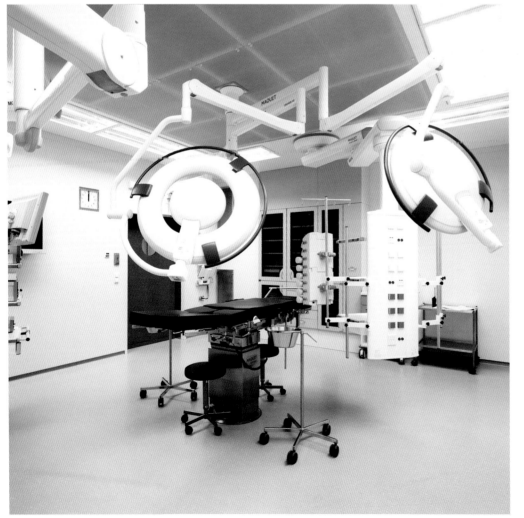

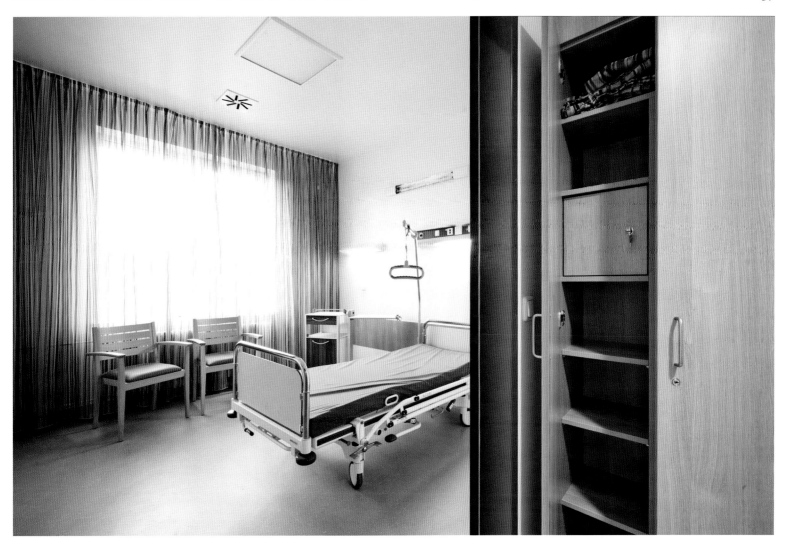

↑ | Standard patient room
↙ | Site plan

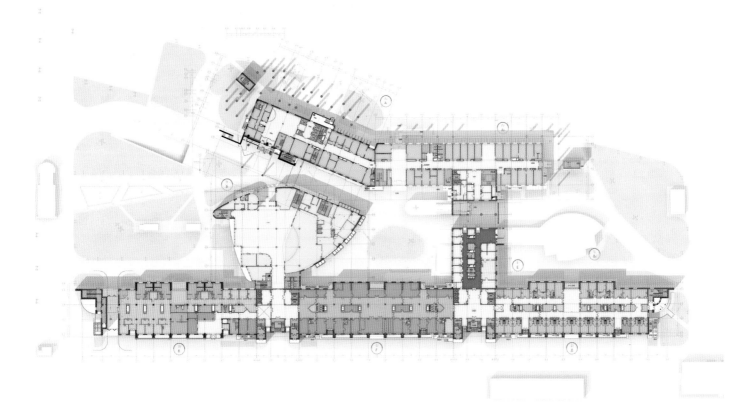

↑ | North side
→ | Stone and glass detail

American British Cowdray
Women's and Children's Hospital

Mexico City

American British Cowdray Women's and Children's Hospital responds to its surroundings and changing environment while embracing functionality. The site shape – semicircular at one end and rectilinear at the other – defined the following geometries. The concept was developed around the curve, subdivided into three distinct architectural elements offering varied solutions to smooth out the connection with the existing building. Where the existing hospital connects with the Women's Center shows a predominance of solids over openings. As the façade moves clockwise toward the north, the glass proportions increase – allowing natural, indirect light into interior spaces while framing site views.

Address: Prolo. Reforma Carlos Graff Fernández 154, 05300 Mexico City, Mexico. **Client:** American British Cowdray. **Completion:** 2008. **Gross floor area:** 14,865 m². **Main materials:** Tepeji marble, glass, steel, concrete, aluminum panels. **Type:** neo-natal, pediatrics. **Building:** new construction. **Treatment areas:** operating rooms. **Operator:** private.

↑ | Patient room
↙ | Floor plan and section

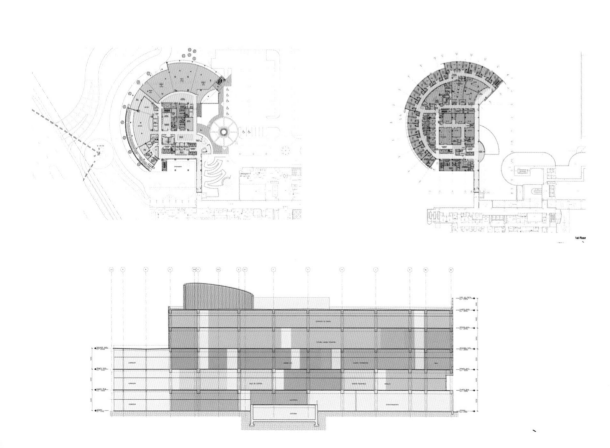

↖ | **Detail**, façade
↓ | **Main lobby**

↑ | **View from below,** with emergency stairs and courtyard
↗ | **Bird's-eye view**
→ | **Extension,** appearing as independent part of the building arrangement

Extension Frauen- und Kopfklinik

Innsbruck

The key concept of this design was the reversal of the sequence of levels designated by the competition program. The service level is positioned as a retreating penultimate level, while the wards are located in an attractive position with lots of natural light from above. The newly added upper levels create a clear silhouette in the Innsbruck cityscape. The four wards are connected by a ring-shaped access corridor, which affords high flexibility in terms of different uses. The ratio of medical floor space to the total useable floor space is valuated as 1:1.96. All patient rooms offer views across the city. The optimization of natural light is achieved by the incorporation of two landscaped courtyards. The service level below the wards is also lit by natural light and houses the administration areas. The emergency staircases also serve the existing building. The tilt of the Alucobond façade, together with the sun shades, emphasizes the floating appearance of the ward level.

Address: Maximilianstraße 35, 6020 Innsbruck, Austria. **Client:** Tilak–Tiroler Landeskrankenanstalten GesmbH. **Completion:** 2008. **Gross floor area:** 6,100 m². **Partners in charge:** Karl Heinz, Jörg Streli. **Main materials:** steel, reinforced concrete, Alucobond façade, aluminum sun shades. **Type:** oncology, bone marrow transplantation, neurology. **Building:** new construction. **Treatment areas:** rehabilitation, physiotherapy. **Operator:** state.

↖ | **View,** of surroundings from courtyard
↑ | **Exterior appearance,** from street
↙ | **Ninth floor plan**

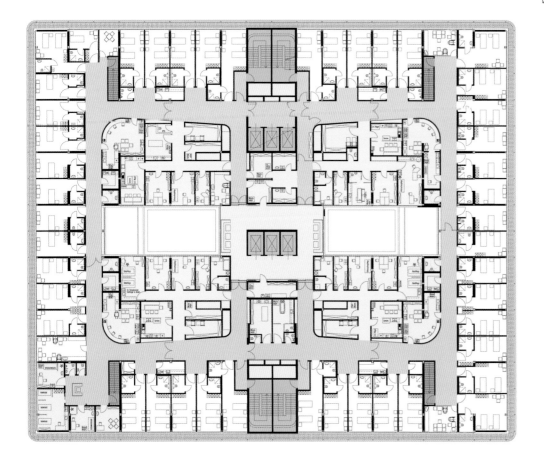

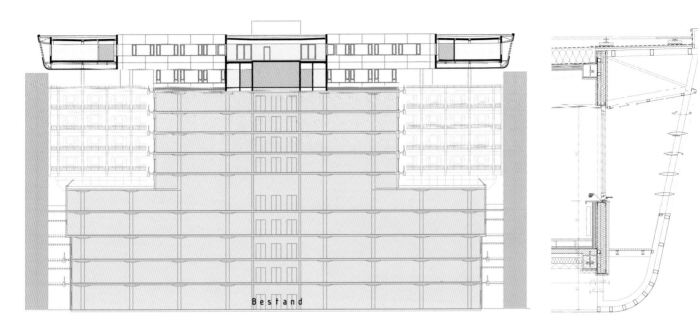

Bestand

↖ | **Section**
↑ | **Detail**, façade extension
↓ | **Patient room**

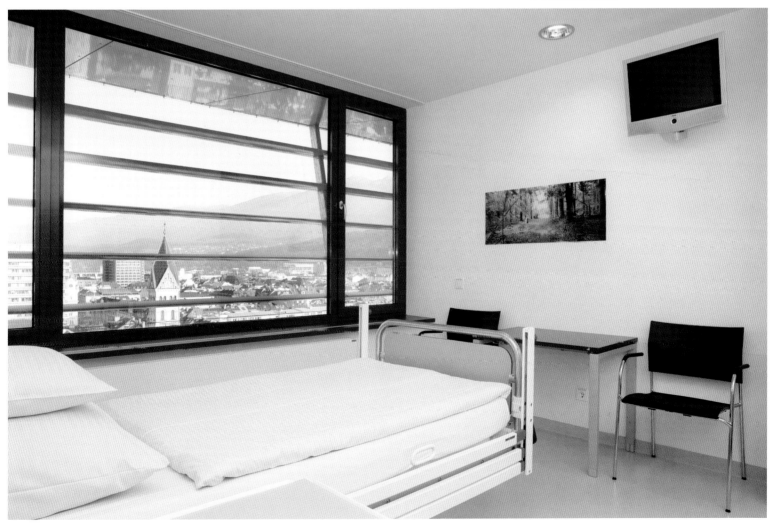

↑ | **Exit to patient garden,** with patient restaurant
→ | **Corridor fifth floor of nursing ward,** with glass lamellae by Bernhard Huber

Robert-Bosch-Hospital

Stuttgart

The upper floors of this cross-shaped five-story building house nursing wards, inpatient treatment areas, operating rooms and the maternity ward, while the ground floor accommodates the more general facilities, such as diagnostics, examination and treatment areas. Supply and waste disposal is located in the partially exposed basement level. Internal organization is finely balanced to optimally accommodate functional medical and operational demands, as well as the personal needs of the patients, visitors and personnel. The use of both natural and artificial materials and colors characterizes the high quality accommodation. Contemporary artwork helps to make this location memorable.

PROJECT FACTS

Address: Auerbachstraße 110, 70376 Stuttgart, Germany. **Client:** Robert-Bosch-Krankenhaus. **Completion:** 2009. **Gross floor area:** 72,000 m². **Landscape architects:** Luz Landschaftsarchitektur. **Architect of entrance area:** Joachim Schürmann. **Type:** cancer, emergency, maternity, pediatrics, cardiology, psychosomatics. **Building:** new construction, renovation. **Treatment areas:** operating rooms. **Operator:** nonprofit.

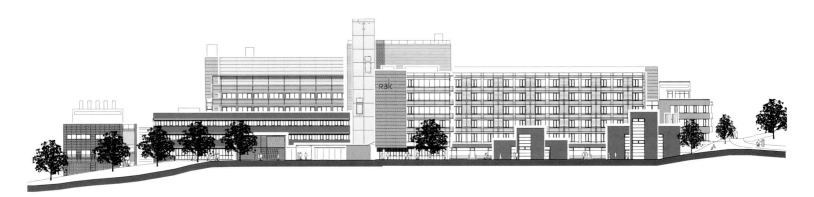

↑ | **Elevation,** from north with main entrance
← | **Artistically designed courtyard,** by Luz
Landschaftarchitektur

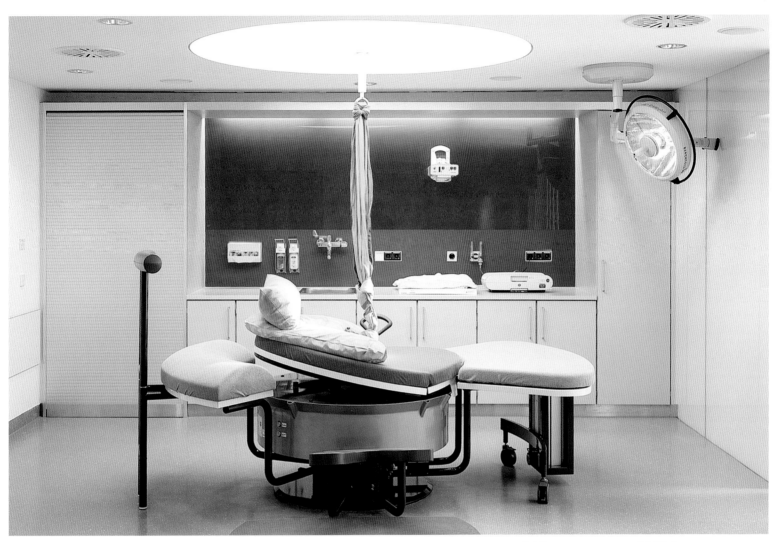

↑ | **Treatment room**, childbirth
↙ | **Site plan**

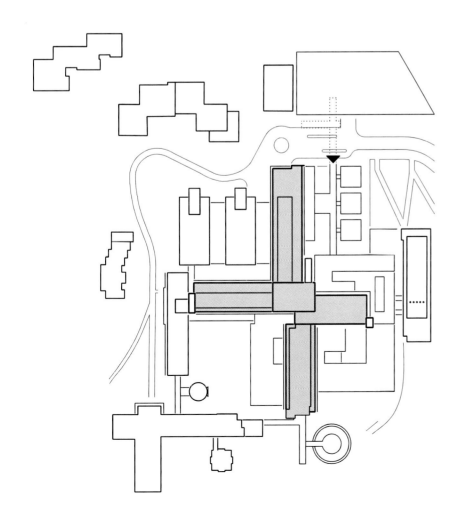

↑ | **Main entrance**
→ | **Entrance lobby**

Foundation Hospital

Forchheim

This building is a specialized hospital that houses an operation and childbirth center with a total of 225 beds. All departments are grouped around a central three-story lobby and are accessed via an open staircase or elevators. This spatial arrangement aids orientation within the 24,000-square-meter building. The innovative technical concept is of particular importance: Well water is used for cooling and thermal power stations reduce the primary energy usage and costly peak consumption periods. The hospital has no heating elements, a strategy that has been made possible by concrete core activation.

PROJECT FACTS

Address: Spitalstraße 4, 91301 Forchheim, Germany. **Client:** Stiftungskrankenhaus Forchheim der Vereinigten Pfründnerstiftungen. **Completion:** 2006. **Gross floor area:** 24,000 m². **Type:** general hospital. **Building:** new construction. **Treatment areas:** operating rooms, rehabilitation, water therapy, physiotherapy. **Operator:** nonprofit.

↑ | Courtyard
↓ | Ground floor plan

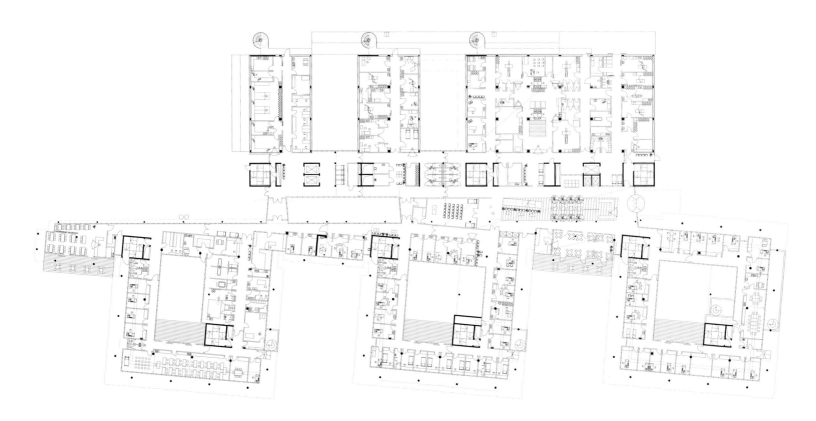

↖ | Site plan
↓ | Patient room

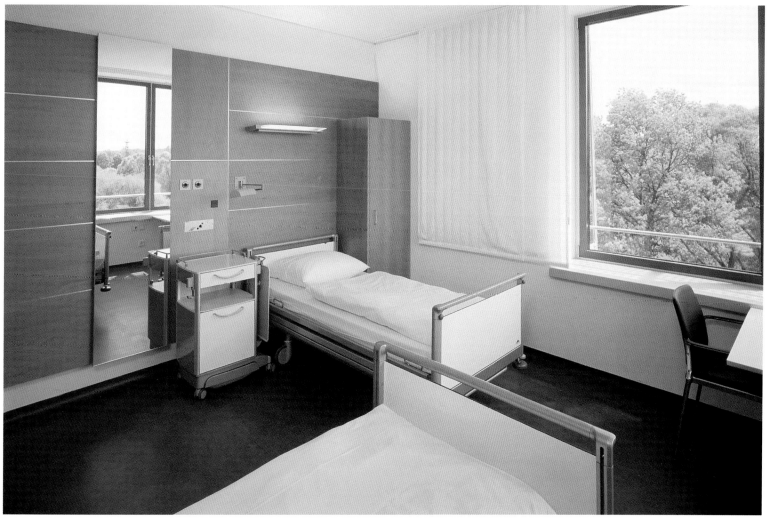

Atelier Thomas Pucher

↑ | **Access road,** through complex
↓ | **Section**

↗ | **Green spaces,** incorporated into design
→ | **Combined elements,** form a coherent whole

Extension of Regional Hospital

Salzburg

This design combines a "double-comb" structure that accommodates treatment and examination rooms with a cross-shaped area dedicated to the ward and nursery departments. The distribution is completed by a final slab that hosts the laboratory and that seamlessly integrates the whole building. The building complex is delimitated toward the train lines by the slabs of the laboratory and the parking garage. The key concept of the general design was to guarantee optimal performance, assuring minimum distances between functions and offering a clear overview of the structure and organization of the building. One of the main ideas was to integrate open green spaces throughout the building that would provide both natural light and a place for quiet contemplation and relaxation for staff and patients.

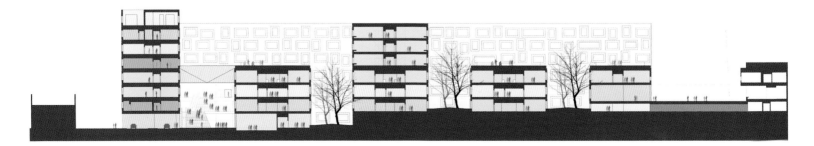

PROJECT FACTS

Address: Müllner Hauptstraße 48, 5020 Salzburg, Austria. **Client:** SALK - Salzburger Landeskliniken. **Completion:** 2015 (first phase). **Gross floor area:** 89,000 m². **Main materials:** concrete, glass. **Type:** emergency, head injury unit. **Building:** new construction. **Operator:** state.

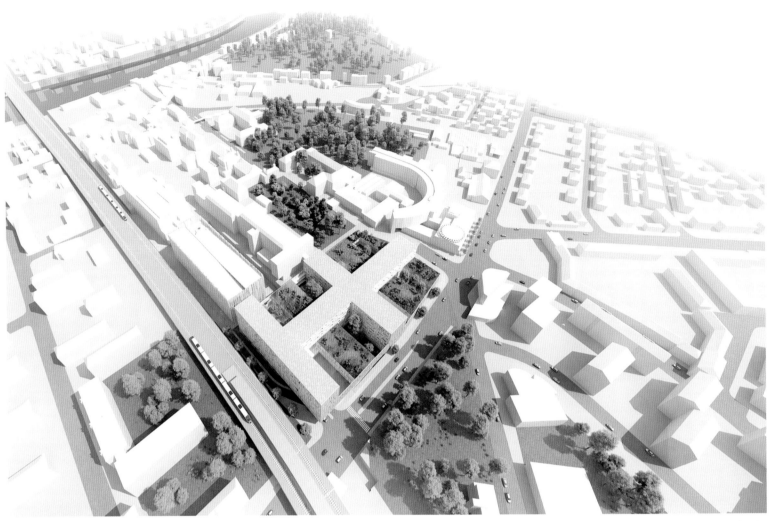

↑ | **Model,** the "pocket parks" are one of the funda-
mental ideas of the project
↙ | **Ground floor plan**

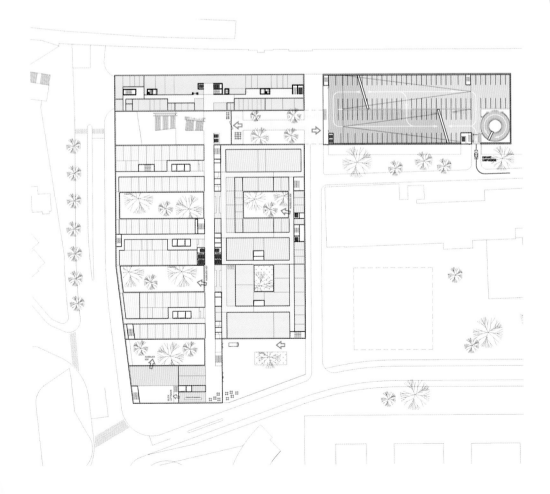

← | Generously glazed areas, allow ample light into building
↓ | Site plan

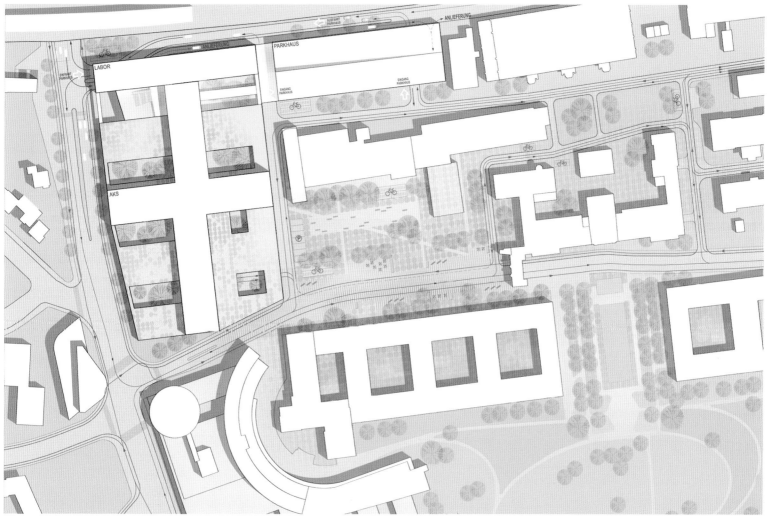

↑ | **Green open spaces,** Bad Homburg clinic
→ | **Large atriums and skylights,** Bad
Homburg clinic

Hochtaunus Clinics

Bad-Homburg and Usingen

Within the framework of a hospital pilot project TMK Architekten · Ingenieure were
awarded the contract for the Hochtaunus Clinics in Bad Homburg (BHG) and Usingen
(USI). These private clinics will be built simultaneously. Both clinics will be constructed
according to the concept of future-oriented development targets and the logistical and
organizational demands, which presented the planners with an extremely complex challenge. The large windows and atriums allow light to flood into the interior giving the
hospitals a bright and welcoming feel.

PROJECT FACTS

Address: Zeppelinstraße 20, 61352 Bad Homburg; Weilburgerstraße 48, 61250 Usingen, Germany. **Client:** Hochtaunus-Kliniken gGmbH. **Completion:** 2014. **Gross floor area:** 63,000 m² (BHG) / 16.890 m² (USI). **Project manager:** Gunnar Dennewill. **Main materials:** aluminum-glass façade. **Type:** emergency, basic diagnostics, radiology. **Building:** new construction. **Treatment areas:** operating rooms, private care rooms, physiotherapy, intensive care. **Operator:** private.

↑ | **Atrium,** Usingen clinic
← | **Ground floor plan,** Usingen

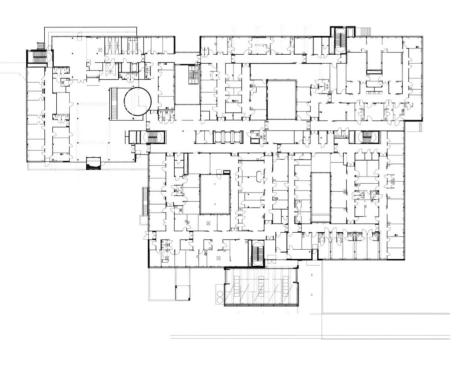

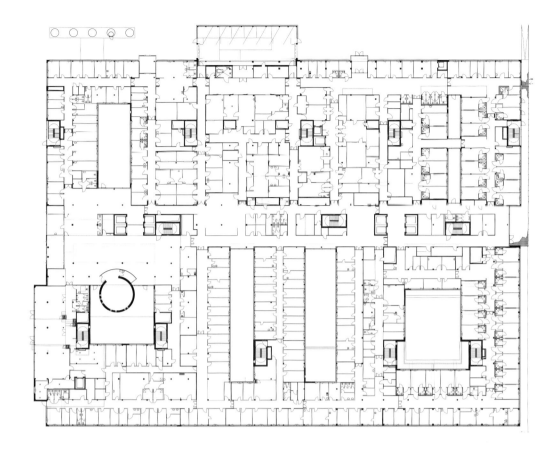

↖ | **Ground floor plan,** Bad Homburg clinic
↓ | **Night view,** Bad Homburg clinic

↑ | **Two-story entrance hall,** linking new and existing buildings
→ | **East façade,** with new adjoining entrance

Schmieder Hospital

Heidelberg

The goal of this project was to unify a heterogeneous structure of single buildings into a complete ensemble that would also rearrange access to the building by means of a clearly defined square. New and old merge together, responding to the topography of the site. The design comprises a two-story entrance hall, which connects the existing and new building components, and a new ward that is positioned at an angle to the entrance. The slightly folded appearance of both buildings sets them apart from the orthogonal existing building. The sunken site provides not only an inviting forecourt as the entrance to the hospital, but also provides access from the entrance hall to the cafeteria on one side and to the wards on the other side.

PROJECT FACTS

Address: Speyererhof, 69117 Heidelberg, Germany. **Client:** Kliniken Schmieder Heidelberg GmbH. **Completion:** 2011. **Gross floor area:** 8,100 m². **Structural engineers:** IB Fischer+Leisering. **Landscape architects:** Rainer Schmidt Landschaftsarchitekten. **Main materials:** wood, aluminum, glass, concrete, exterior insulation finishing system (EIFS). **Type:** pediatrics, neurology. **Building:** new construction. **Operator:** private.

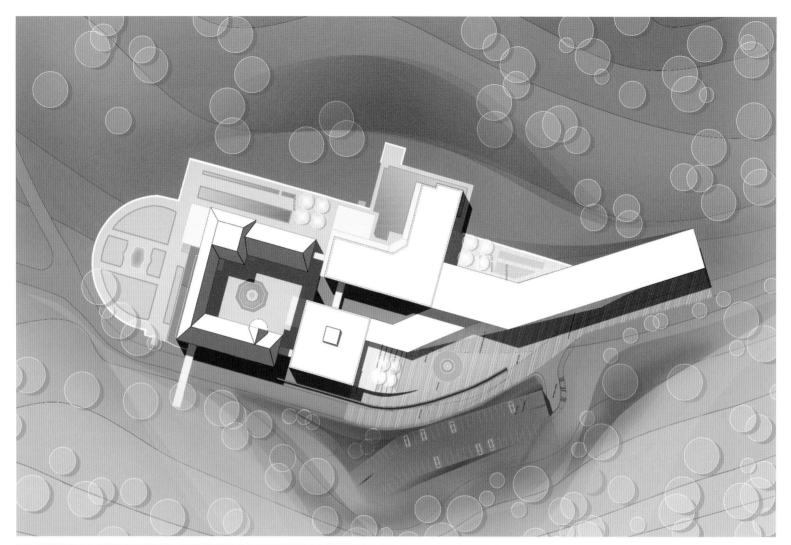

↑ | **Site plan**
← | **Nurses' station,** on third floor

← | **Patient room,** with view of valley
↓ | **View from west,** new ward building

↑ | **Light atrium**, on operating room level
→ | **Doors of "weaning rooms"**

New Intensive Care and Bronchology Unit

Essen

The West German Lung Center at the university clinic in Essen – called "Ruhrland Clinic" – initiated the construction of an extension which houses special intensive care units for artificial respiration and a bronchology unit. Two bridges to the south of the complex connect the new extension to the existing building. The use of state-of-the-art technology and comfortable patient rooms characterizes the appearance of the new building. Patients are weaned off respiratory machines in specialized "weaning rooms". A Patient Data Management System (PDMS) has been introduced to allow paperless management of patient records. The operating rooms are paneled with colored glass and provide a high standard of hygiene and lighting options. The telemedical system and the endoscope washing and disinfecting in the cold process method are considered remarkable parts of the bronchology unit.

PROJECT FACTS

Address: Tüschener Weg 40, 45239 Essen, Germany. **Client:** Ruhrlandklinik, Westdeutsches Lungen-zentrum am Universitätsklinikum Essen gGmbH. **Completion:** 2012. **Gross floor area:** 4,150 m². **Main materials:** reinforced concrete skeleton structure, glass, exterior insulation finishing system. **Type:** bron-chology, intensive care with respiratory "weaning rooms". **Building:** new construction. **Treatment areas:** operating rooms. **Operator:** state.

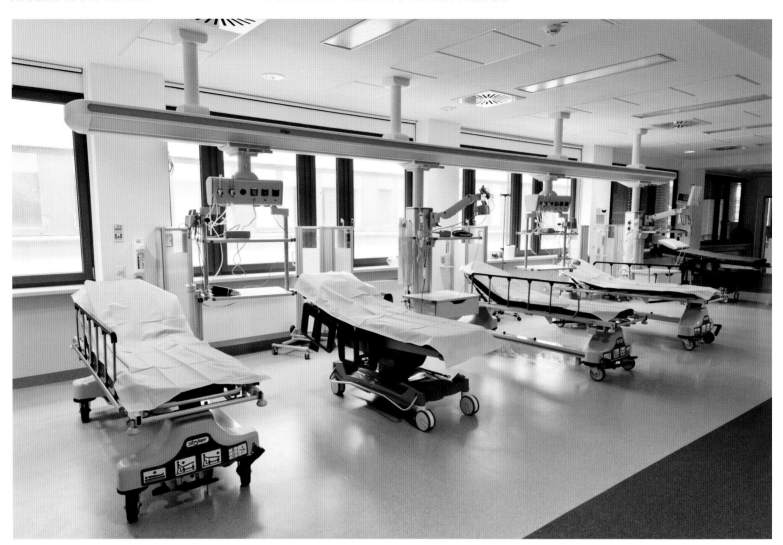

↑ | **Recovery area**
↙ | **Ground floor plan**

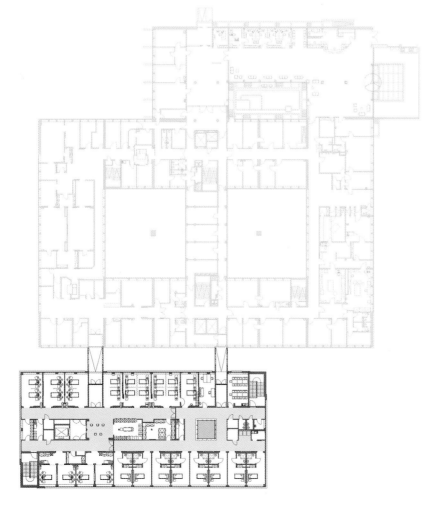

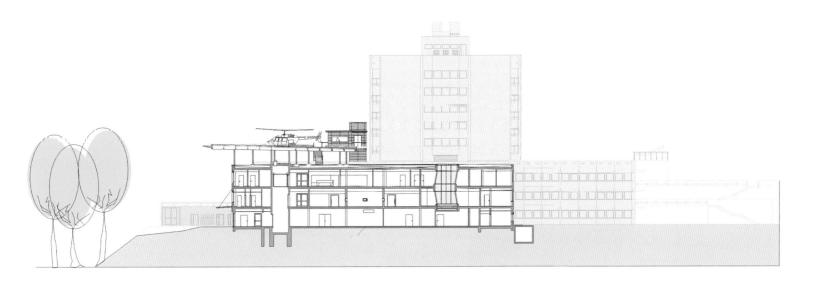

↑ | **Section**
↓ | **Access corridor,** rooms on operating room level

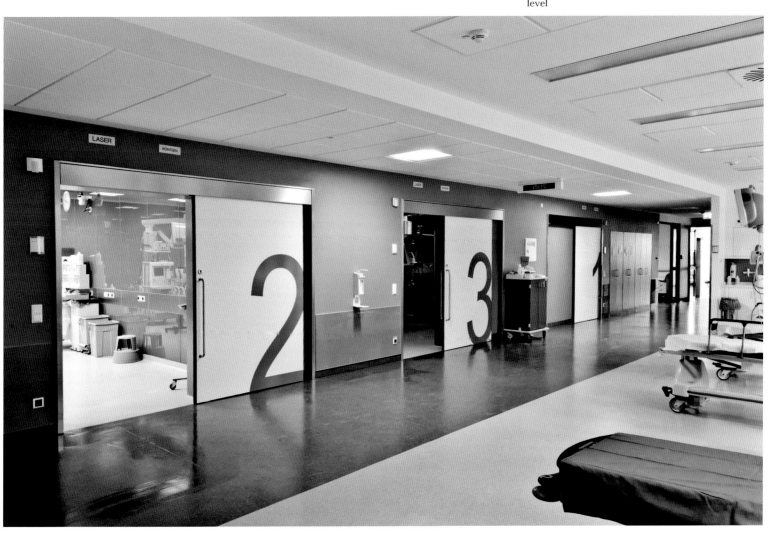

↑ | **Detail**, façade
↗ | **East façade**, exterior view
→ | **Façade**

Sana Ohre Hospital

Haldensleben

The Sana Ohre Hospital is located on an attractive rural site at the western edge of the town of Haldensleben. Within the framework of the hospital-wide master plan, a concept was developed to concentrate all functions in one centralized location and to optimize operational procedures. This included comprehensive reorganization of the interior circulation, as well as refurbishment of the existing building. This was also extended by two new wards, oriented toward the south and housing a total of eight nursing stations. The examination and treatment areas were completed with a new intensive care unit and diagnostics and endoscopy rooms.

PROJECT FACTS

Address: Kiefholzstraße 27, 39340 Haldensleben, Germany. **Client:** Sana Ohre-Klinikum. **Completion:** 2008. **Gross floor area:** 19,843 m². **Main materials:** reinforced concrete. **Type:** emergency medicine, neo-natal, children. **Building:** new construction, renovation. **Treatment areas:** operating rooms, physiotherapy. **Operator:** private.

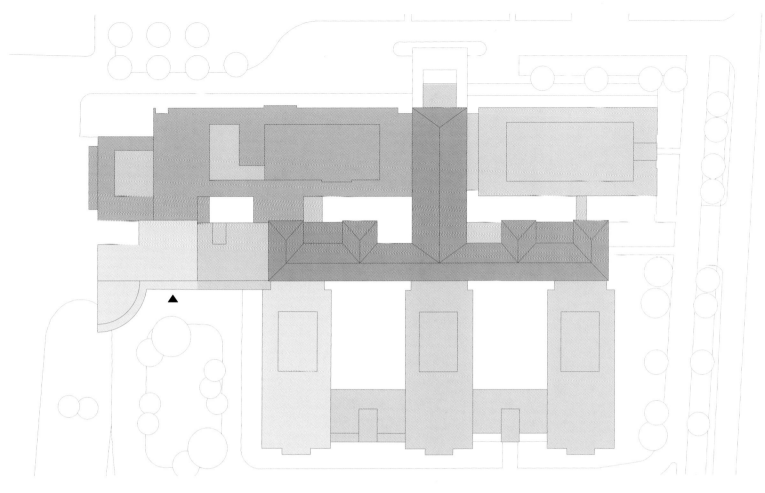

←←| Patient room
↑ | Site plan
↓ | Brightly lit corridor

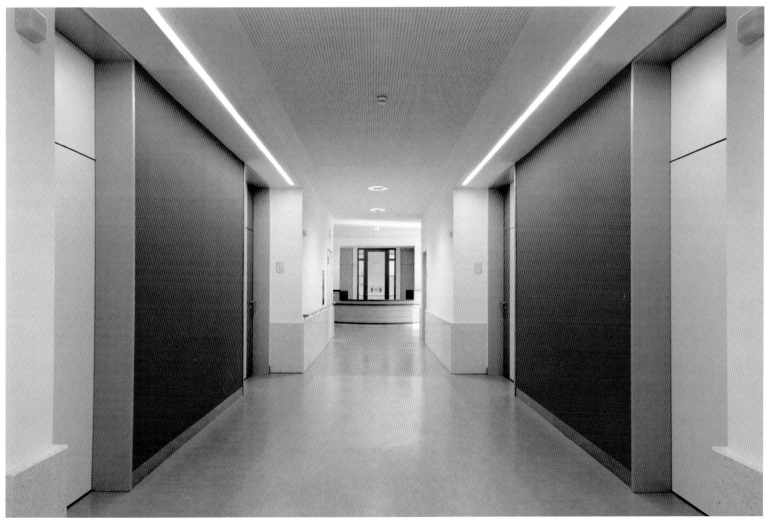

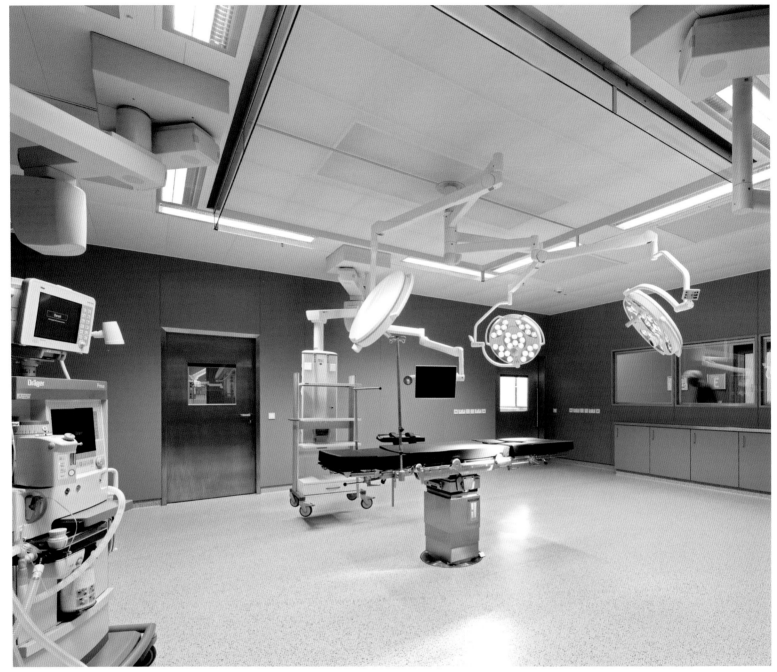

↑ | **Operating room**
↗ | **Waiting room,** basement
→ | **Recovery area**

Central Operation and Coordination Center

Dortmund

Dortmund hospital's Central Operation and Coordination Center is the second largest local hospital in Germany and optimizes the functions of a modern hospital. A functional infrastructure was created by the compact organization of the new building and by establishing links between the new and existing building components. Visitors are guided through the original entrance of the main building and to the new building sections via a light-flooded access corridor. A large hall serves as the information and reception area. The hospital has 12 operating rooms and also houses a cardiac care center, intensive care unit and maternity ward. The building is 150 meters long and 50 meters wide, with five stories that can be extended in the future if necessary.

Address: Beurhausstraße 40, 44137 Dortmund, Germany. **Client:** Klinikum Dortmund gGmbH. **Completion:** 2012. **Gross floor area:** 21,000 m². **Project manager:** Oliver Rauch. **Main materials:** concrete, glass façade. **Type:** operation and diagnostics center. **Building:** new construction. **Treatment areas:** operating rooms, clinical diagnostics, gynecological clinic, obstetrics. **Operator:** state.

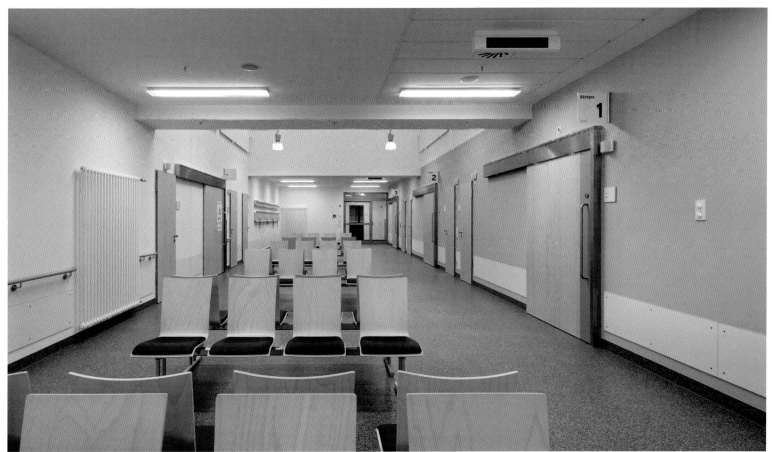

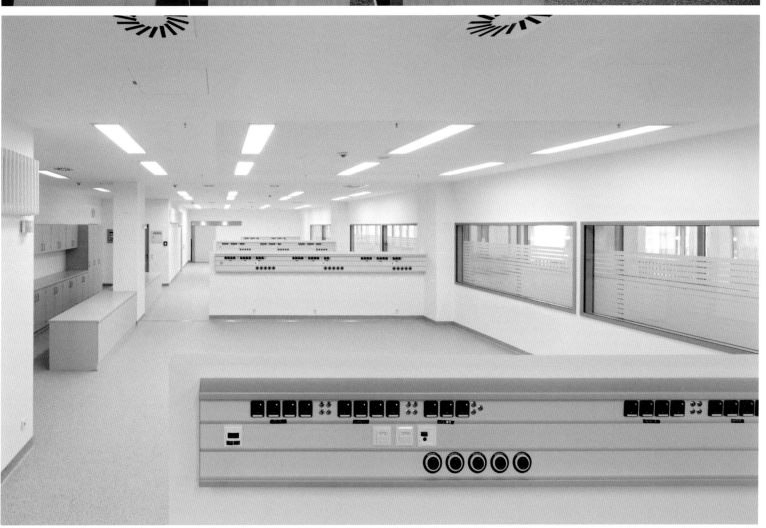

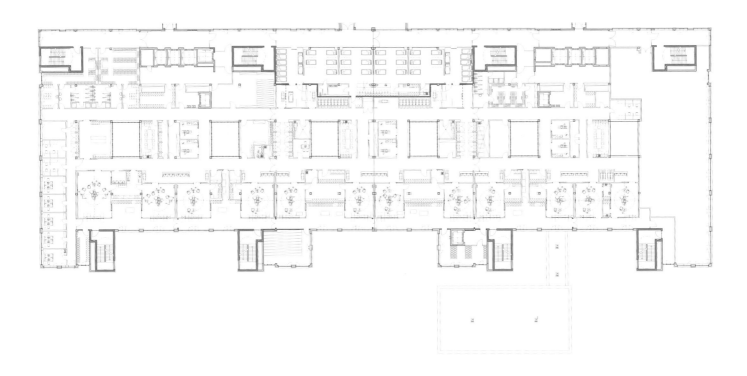

↑ | Ground floor plan
← | Sterile corridor

← | **Corridor,** second floor
↓ | **Basement plan**

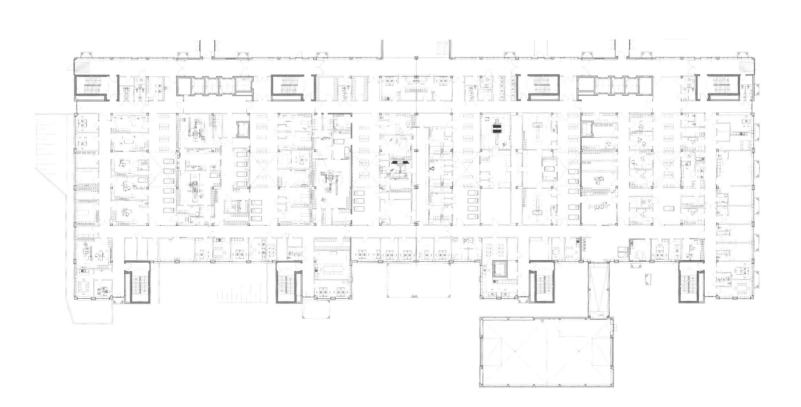

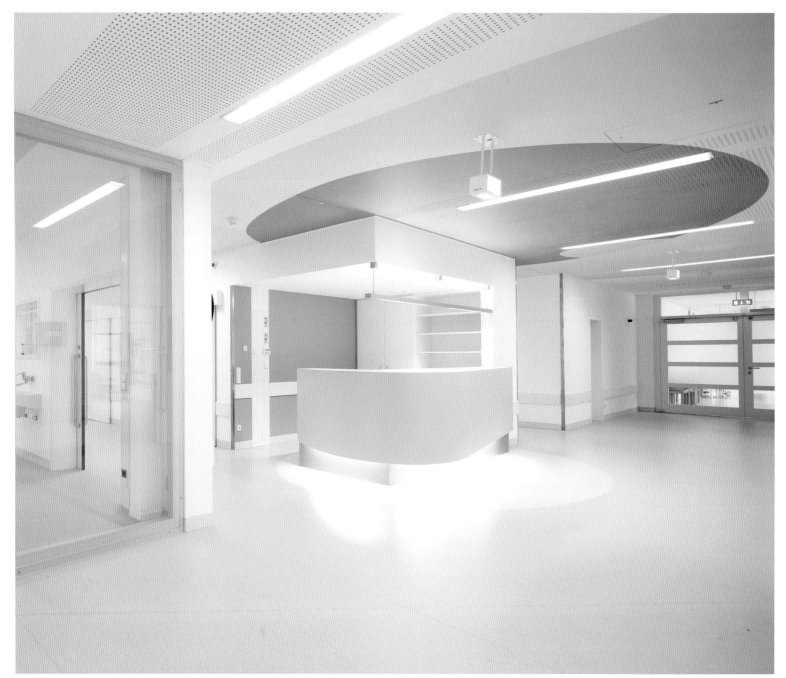

↑ | **Children's ward,** intensive care
↗ | **Exterior perspective**
→ | **Emergency ward,** with view across the city

St. Elisabeth Hospital

Ravensburg

The St. Elisabeth Hospital is organized into four blocks linearly arranged along a four-story access hall. This organization allows for a clear layout and makes orientation much easier. The ward design is envisaged as a pavilion construction. The 36 patient beds in each station are positioned around daylit interior courtyards. Patient accommodation will be provided solely in either single or two-bed rooms. A centrally-located base for nursing personnel has been designed as an open reception desk; optimally positioned to ease operational processes. Double stations are located opposite each other and these can be joined together, allowing them to be operated as a single unit.

Address: Elisabethenstraße 15, 88212 Ravensburg, Germany. **Client:** Landkreis Ravensburg, Eigenbetrieb IKP. **Completion:** 2012 (phase 1). **Gross floor area:** 48,100 m². **Artistic room decoration:** Hannes Trüjen/painting placement. **Main materials:** reinforced concrete, glass, ceramic façade. **Type:** cancer, pediatrics, maternity, emergency. **Building:** new construction, renovation. **Treatment areas:** operating rooms, physiotherapy. **Operator:** state.

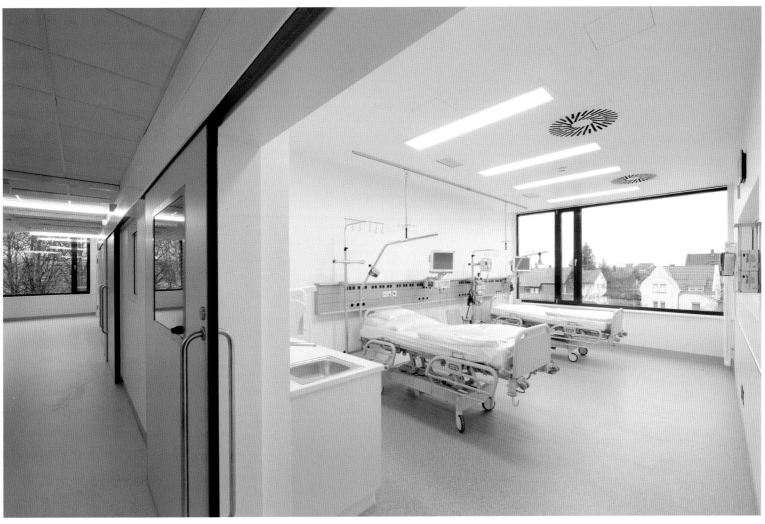

↑ | **Treatment room,** intensive care
← | **Site plan**

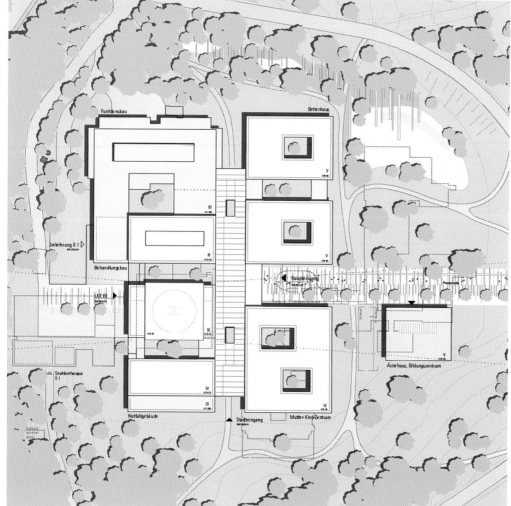

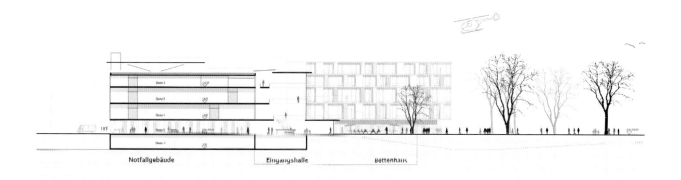

↑ | Sections
↓ | Interior perspective

↑ | **Exterior,** center specifically for outpatients
↗ | **Main entrance,** to the well-equipped center
→ | **Fourth floor operating room,** providing
views of ancient Green Timbers Forest

Jim Pattison Outpatient Care and Surgery Center

Surrey

The Jim Pattison Outpatient Care and Surgery Center is a stand-alone outpatient facility for patients who need medical care or treatment, but do not require an overnight stay in hospital. The center is equipped with over 100 examination and treatment rooms, ten procedural rooms and six operating rooms; offering over 50 specialized health clinics and programs. The Public Private Partnership project is designed to meet LEED Gold standards and embraces the latest thinking in health care implementation and medical treatment. Conceived as a place of healing and community, this facility provides a safe, secure and welcoming environment for the whole family, irrespective of age or background.

PROJECT FACTS

Address: 9750, 140 Street, Surrey, V3T 0G9 Canada. **Client:** Fraser Health Authority. **Completion:** 2011. **Gross floor area:** 16,620 m². **Main materials:** concrete, steel. **Type:** cancer, neo-natal, pediatrics, outpatient facility. **Building:** new construction. **Staff areas:** coffee shop, offices. **Treatment areas:** operating rooms, diagnostic imaging, rehabilitation, physiotherapy. **Operator:** state.

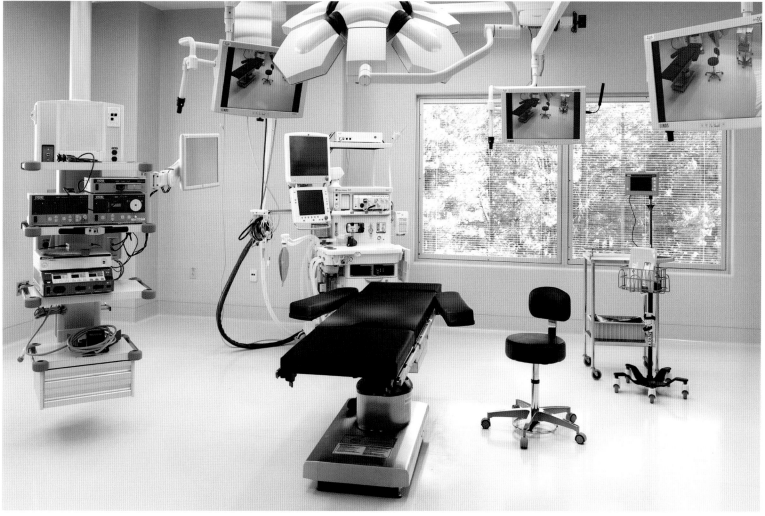

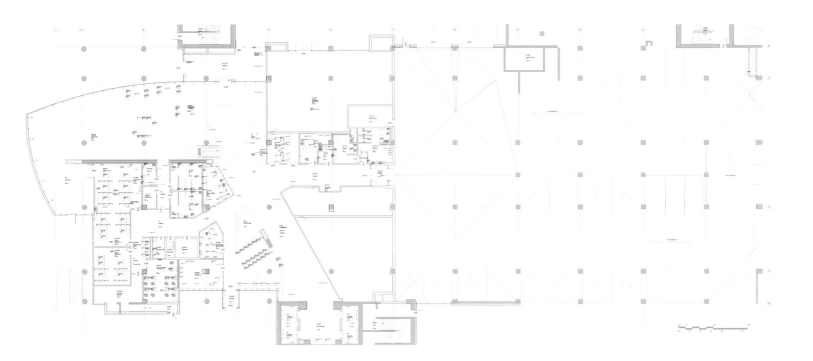

↑ | **Ground floor plan,** including cafeteria
↓ | **Evolving tree graphic,** assists in wayfinding

← | **Cafeteria,** centralized and easily accessible
↓ | **Second floor plan,** including medical imaging

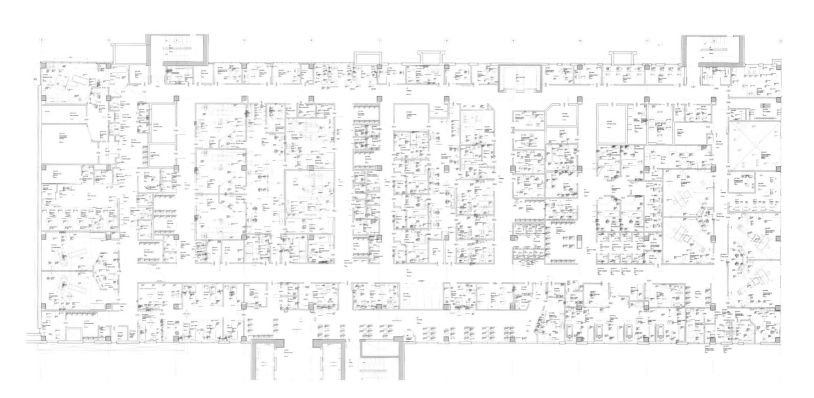

↑ | **Main view,** street
↗ | **Front façade**
→ | **Lobby,** waiting room

Righospitalet Expansion

Copenhagen

A team of 3XN architects, Aarhus Architects, Nickl & Partner Architekten, Grontmij and Kirstine Jensen Studio won the competition for the expansion of Copenhagen's main hospital, Rigshospitalet. The building's shape is characterized by a series of folded V-structures together with a transversal fast track. The structuring provides space for five atriums that will serve both as comfortable lounge areas and points of orientation, making way-finding easy and logical. The shape of the building ensures an interior that is characterized by lots of daylight and views of both the park and city. The integration of sustainable building solutions, gardens and green walls both inside and outside was a key focus of the design process. The building has nine floors up against the existing hospital complex and just four facing the street. The façade of glass and light natural stone is angled so that it is partially self-shading and visually adapts to the area's existing building façades.

PROJECT FACTS

Address: Blegdamsvej, Copenhagen, Denmark. **Client:** Rigshospitalet organized under the Capital Region of Denmark. **Completion:** 2017. **Gross floor area:** 68,000 m². **Main materials:** glass, natural stone. **Type:** center for head injuries and orthopedics. **Building:** new construction. **Operator:** state.

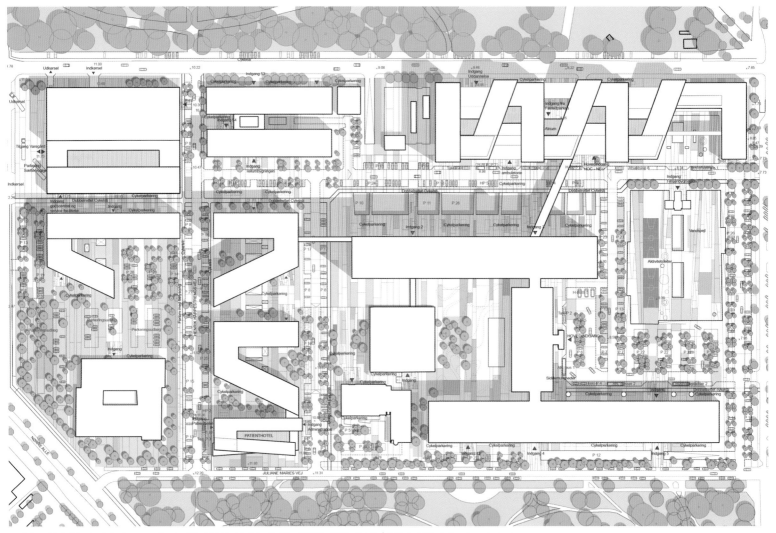

↑ | **Site plan**
← | **Bird's-eye view**, at night

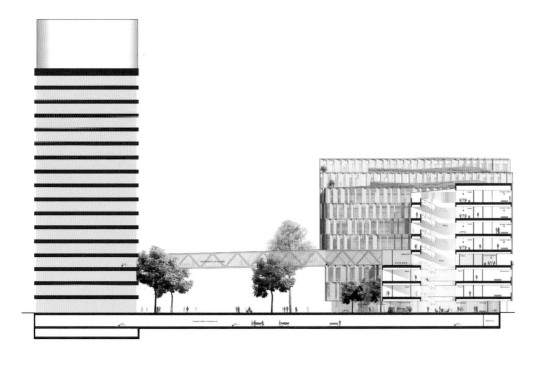

↖ | **Section**
↓ | **Bird's-eye view,** green rooftops

↑ | **Main entrance,** connection to clinics
↗ | **View,** toward Bergstraße
→ | **Hall,** staircase

Health Center

Bochum

The Augusta Clinics in Bochum have a multifunctional health center that is spread across six levels and has around 7,300 square meters of rentable space for medical practices, therapists and other service providers from the medical sector. The building comprises four full levels; one recessed, staggered level, and a basement level. In addition to the radiotherapy center with two linear accelerators, a dialysis center with 65 dialysis stations, there is also an oncology outpatient clinic with 32 available treatment places. The location is situated in close proximity to the Augusta clinics and is directly linked to them via a pedestrian bridge. A generously glazed, three-story hall marks the entrance.

Address: Bergstraße 25, 44791 Bochum, Germany. **Client:** Augusta Kliniken Bochum. **Completion:** 2010.
Gross floor area: 10,270 m². **Main materials:** reinforced concrete, high pressure laminate façade panels.
Building: new construction. **Operator:** nonprofit.

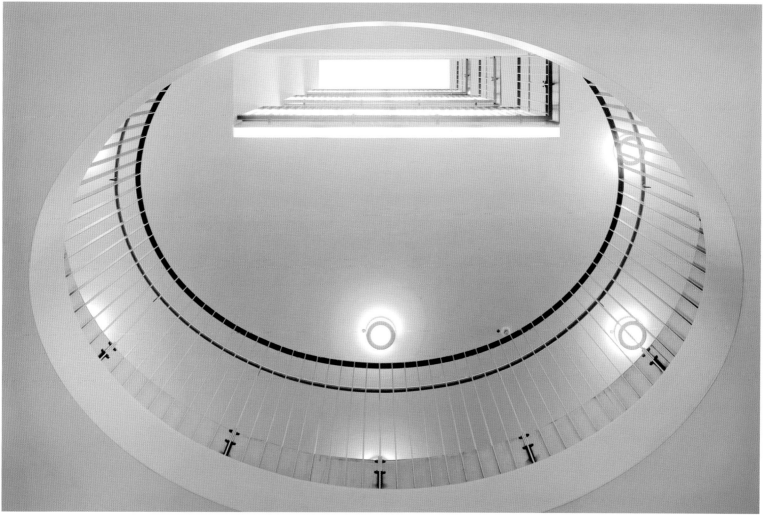

↑ | **Waiting room,** for radiotherapy
↙ | **Site plan**

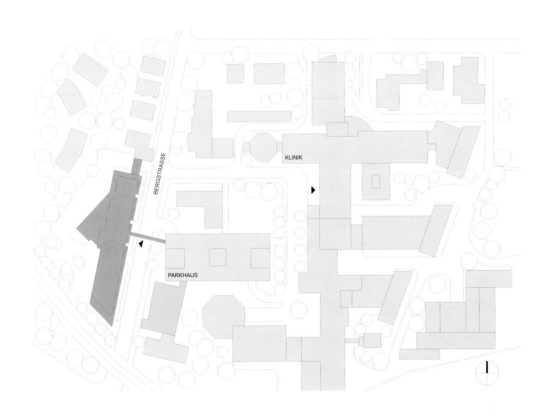

← | West view
↓ | Linear accelerator

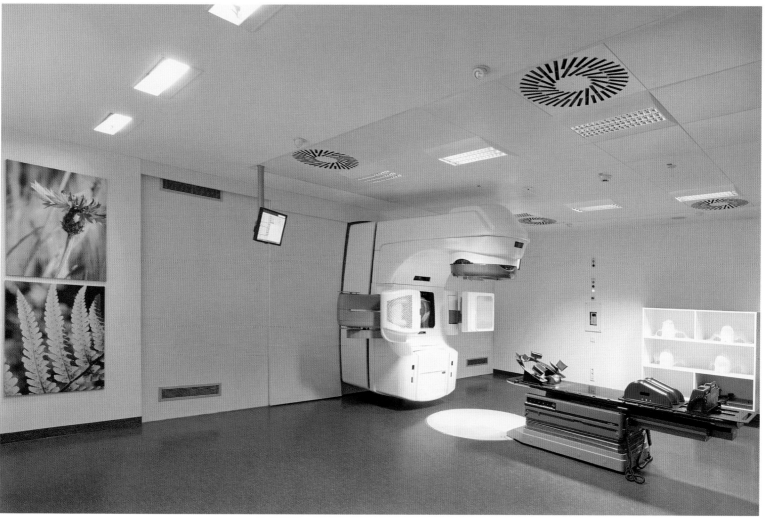

TASH –
Taller de Arquitectura

↑ | **Main view,** pediatrics building
↗ | **Renal institute and hospitalization spaces,** adjacent to hospital
→ | **Main entrance,** hall courtyard

New Panama City Hospital

Clayton

This project is configured as a city, it is not a single building but a complex, keeping the capacity of total intercommunication between different buildings in a way that benefits from the different synergies, general systems, logistics, production systems, waste disposal, etc., avoiding element duplicities and improving the performance, thus giving sense to the concept of hospital city that is at the core of the project. Due to the different needs of a modern hospital as well as other physical conditions such as orientation and lot location, the different elements of the hospital city are distributed following a linear model. This model develops throughout an axis that connects all the components together.

Address: Calle de la Floresta, Clayton, Panama. **Client:** Caja de Seguro social de Panamá. **Completion:** ongoing. **Gross floor area:** 220,000 m². **Main materials:** concrete, pre-cast concrete blocks, steel, glass. **Type:** cancer, psychiatric, emergency medicine, neo-natal, pediatrics. **Building:** new construction. **Treatment areas:** operating rooms, rehabilitation, water therapy, physiotherapy. **Operator:** state.

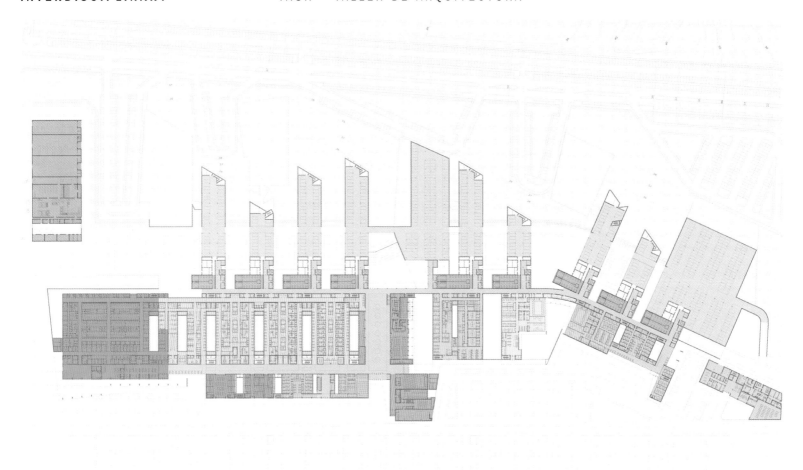

↑ | **Ground floor plan**
← | **Patient hotel,** and pediatrics building

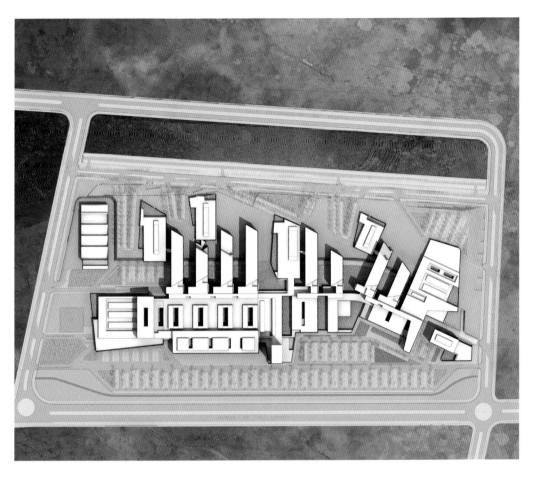

↖ | **Bird's-eye view**
↓ | **Main entrance,** and administration tower

Arcass Freie Architekten

↑ | **Entrance,** front view
↘ | **Section**

↗ | **Bird's-eye view**
→ | **Courtyard,** framed by transparent building elements

Diakonie Klinikum Social Welfare Clinic

Stuttgart

A quiet green courtyard is framed by transparent building elements, creating light-filled rooms and a comfortable atmosphere that aids fast convalescence. The patient rooms are all oriented toward the courtyard garden. The rooms and the buildings as a whole convey a hotel-like atmosphere and the upper floors offer stunning view across Stuttgart. Wilhelm Hospital is a historical listed building and the adjacent new buildings are connected to each other via an interior "patient street", this corridor provides access to all areas of both the existing building and new elements. The juxtaposition of old and new reflects the self-perception of the operators: Christian tradition combined with advanced medicine.

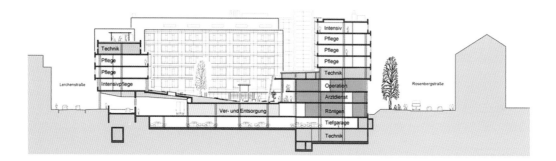

Address: Rosenbergstraße 38, 70176 Stuttgart, Germany. **Client:** Diakonie-Klinikum Stuttgart gGmbH. **Completion:** 2008. **Gross floor area:** 49,050 m². **Main materials:** glass, wood, brick. **Type:** cancer, emergency, orthopedics. **Building:** new construction, renovation. **Treatment areas:** operating rooms, physiotherapy. **Operator:** nonprofit.

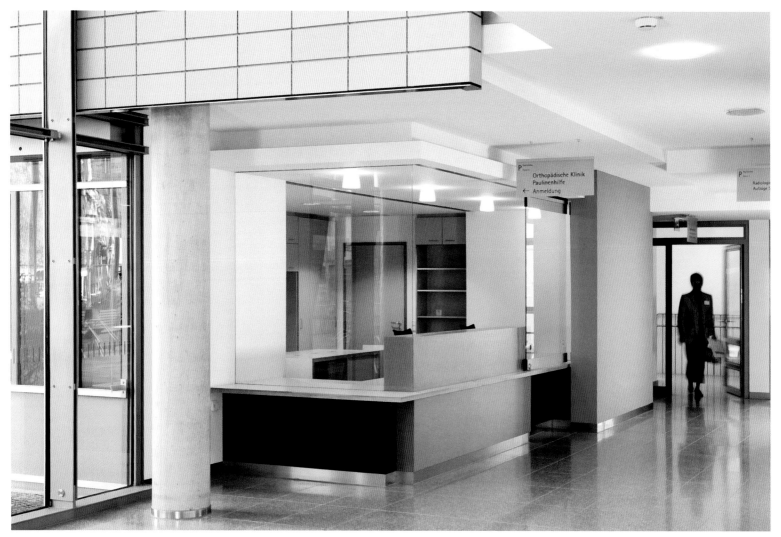

↑ | **Nurses' station**
↙ | **Aerial view**

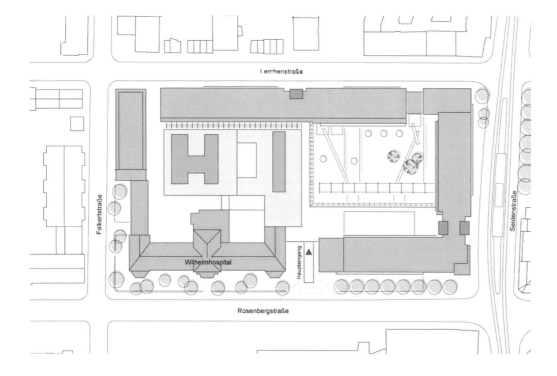

← | **Corridor,** leading to operating rooms
↓ | **First floor plan**

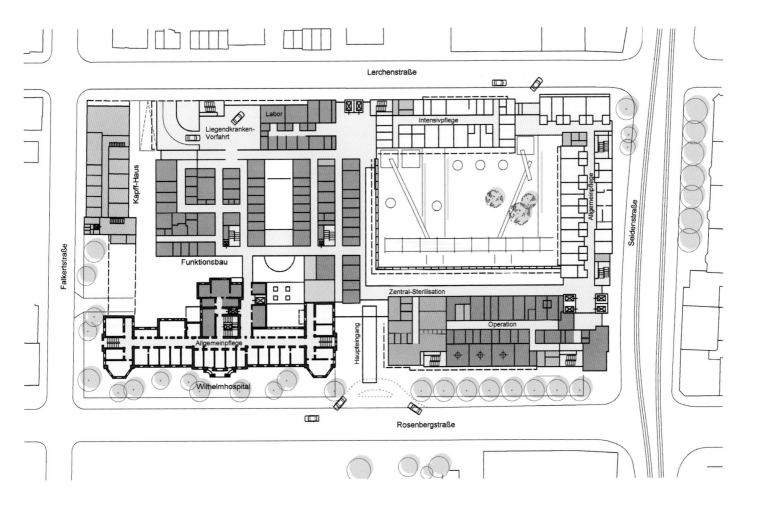

↑ | **Hospital building**, in context
↘ | **Cross section**, west-east

↗ | **Patient room**
→ | **Main entrance**

New Gemini Hospital

Den Helder

Planetree and the living building concept were key themes for the design of this new hospital. Planetree strives to create a pleasant environment for both patients and staff whilst the living building concept ensures that a building can shrink or expand in order to meet demand. The reference to the surrounding dunes is reinforced by the façade cladding, which is composed of perforated metal panels with images of the surrounding dunes. The blocks have a north south lengthwise orientation allowing for beautiful views from the rooms. The use of colors and natural materials in the interior design give it a more welcoming hotel ambiance rather than the clinical atmosphere typically associated with hospitals. The patient rooms also have rooming-in facilities so that close family can stay with the patient overnight.

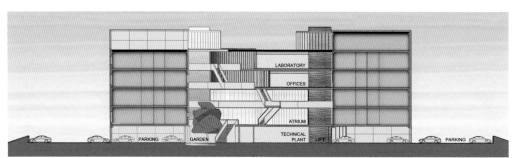

PROJECT FACTS

Address: Den Helder, The Netherlands. **Client:** Gemini Ziekenhuis. **Completion:** 2015. **Gross floor area:** 25,000 m². **Main materials:** powder-coated perforated metal panels, glazed curtain walling. **Type:** cancer, emergency medicine, neo-natal, pediatrics. **Building:** new construction. **Treatment areas:** operating rooms, rehabilitation, physiotherapy. **Operator:** nonprofit.

↑ | **Detail**, façade
← | **Façade development image**

← | **Interior,** filled with light from skylights
↓ | **Site plan and elevation**

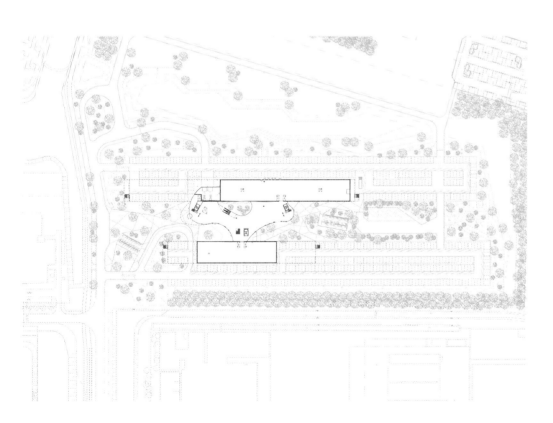

Corea & Moran Arquitectura
Pich–Aguilera Architects

↑ | **Aerial view**
↗ | **View,** from highway
→ | **Rehabilitation area**

Hospital Sant Joan de Reus

Reus

This project is presented as a major horizontal unit. The six-story main building rests on light wells, giving them a floating appearance. These volumes are linked to a large public circulation area. The project is organized into two circulation axes or streets. The medical circulation axis is located at the north end of the site where the entrances and exits of the parking lot and the technical logistics sector will be built. The public circulation axis, located to the south of the site, opens onto a new pedestrian walkway. The façade plane that covers the whole building is bent over, optically reducing the physical presence of the building and increasing its effect.

PROJECT FACTS

Address: Avenida del Dr. Josep Laporte, 2, 43204 Reus, Spain. **Client:** Innova Grup d'Empreses Municipals, S.L., Servei Català de la Salut. **Completion:** 2010. **Gross floor area:** 104,910 m². **Structural engineers:** BIS Arquitectes. **Main materials:** concrete, steel. **Type:** cancer, emergency medicine, neo-natal, pediatrics. **Building:** new construction. **Treatment areas:** operating rooms, rehabilitation, physiotherapy. **Operator:** state.

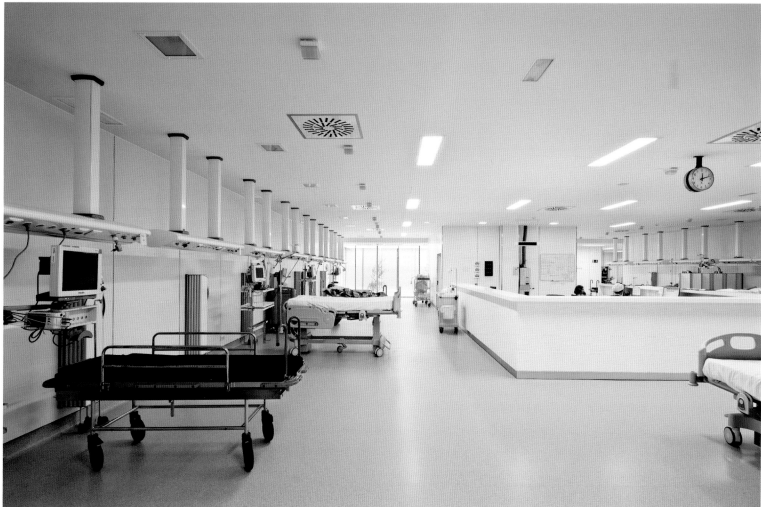

↑ | Site plan
← | Main entrance

↑ | **Interior plaza**
↓ | **Ground floor plan**

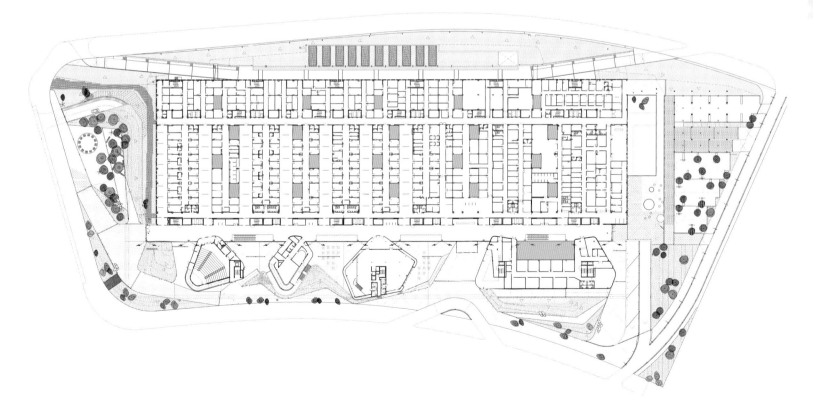

Sander Hofrichter
Architekten Partnerschaft

↑ | **New building,** main view
↘ | **Elevation**

↗ | **Atrium,** allows daylight to flood into interior
→ | **Waiting area**

University Medical Clinic

Tübingen

Following the demolition of the existing building, it was necessary to design a modern, multifunctional building that would integrate a large part of the medical clinic. The ward to the west of the medical clinic creates space for 145 patients to be accommodated in either single or double rooms. The patient rooms are spread across four stories oriented toward the large façade surfaces. Large glazed areas communicate the willingness of the personnel to cater for the individual needs of the patients and also allow continuous view through large parts of the ward. The patient rooms appear both large and welcoming, thanks to the high windows and light natural surfaces, as well as the cleverly integrated storage elements.

Address: Am Schnarrenberg, 72076 Tübingen, Germany. **Client:** Land Baden-Württemberg represented by Vermögen und Bau Baden-Württemberg. **Completion:** 2007. **Gross floor area:** 13,880 m². **Main materials:** reinforced concrete, insulation materials. **Type:** cancer, emergency medicine. **Building:** new construction. **Operator:** state. **Signage:** two interior courtyards aid orientation.

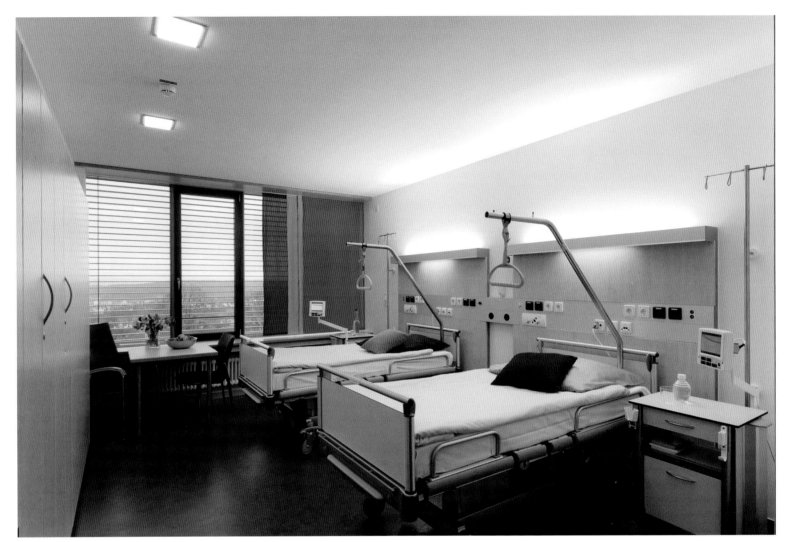

↑ | Two-bed patient room
↓ | Third floor plan

↑ | Access to organizational areas
↓ | Sixth floor plan

↑ | **Main entrance**
→ | **Design concept,** based on the idea of a tree house

New Mother and Child Center –
Caritas Hospital

Bad Mergentheim

This building is characterized by the idea of a tree house, which was the central design concept. The first floor cantilevers out over the front of the building and is supported by a number of stilts, giving it the appearance of a tree house resting on branches. This impression is emphasized by the façade design and continued in the interior of the hospital. Lots of natural daylight, simple pathways and a homely atmosphere help to calm patients' anxiety and reinforce trust. Energy-saving aspects, which play an increasingly important role in operational processes, have been implemented through the use of modern energy technologies. Sustainable techniques include solar panels for heating service water, an air-water heat pump and a photovoltaic system, as well as heat/cool recovery by a central air supplier and extractor.

PROJECT FACTS

Address: Uhlandstraße 7, 97980 Bad Mergentheim, Germany. **Client:** Caritas-Krankenhaus Bad Mergentheim gGmbH. **Completion:** 2011. **Gross floor area:** 6,020 m². **Artist:** Hannes Trüjen/painting placement. **Main materials:** linoleum, fiber cement boards, exterior insulation finishing system. **Type:** maternity, pediatrics. **Building:** new construction. **Treatment areas:** operating rooms, physiotherapy. **Operator:** nonprofit.

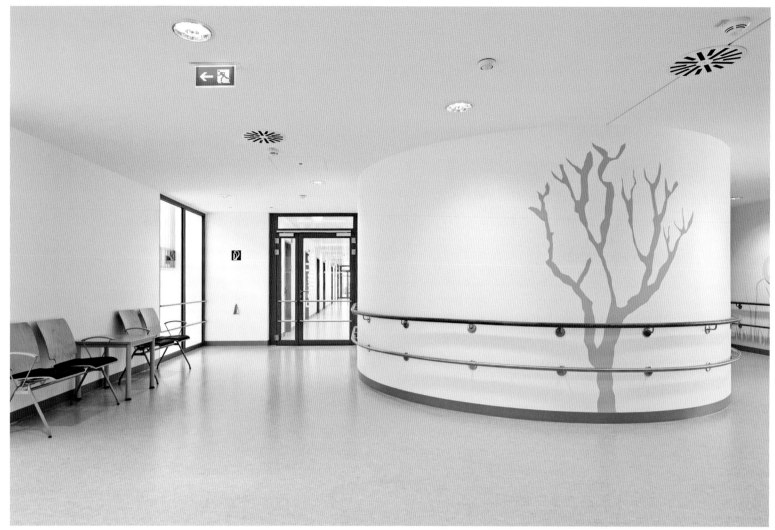

↑ | **Entrance,** to examination and treatment areas
↓ | **First floor plan**

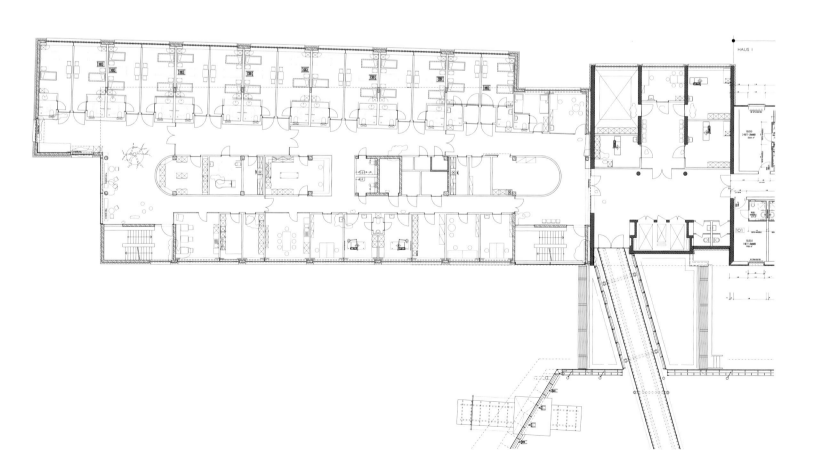

↑ | East elevation
↓ | Nurses' station

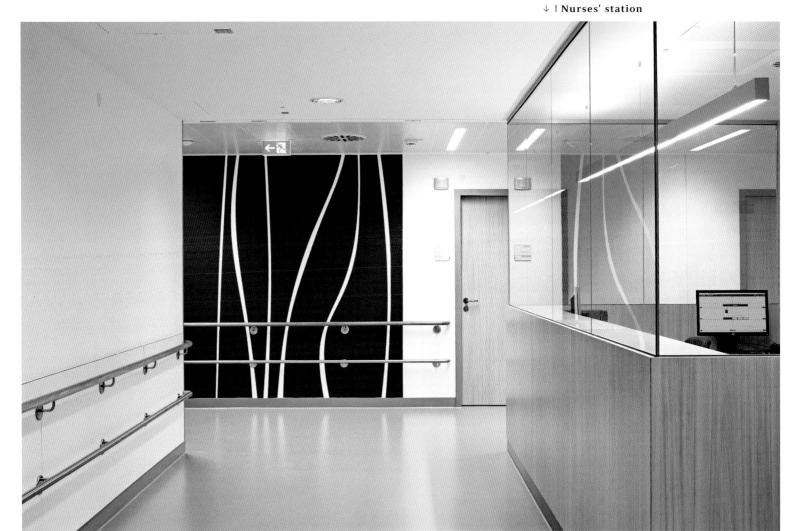

tönies + schroeter + jansen
freie architekten

↑ | **Main view,** building volume
→ | **Glazed access corridor,** with red units

Conservative Medicine
Johannes-Gutenberg University

Mainz

This clinic for conservative medicine is one of Mainz University's most modern build-ings, housing the medical clinics 1–3, the radiology clinic, the institute for clinical chem-istry and laboratory technology, as well as research laboratories. This state-of-the-art clinic is process-oriented, functional, economical in terms of the functional areas, and patient-friendly in the ward areas. The differing volumes, as well as the position and orientation of the buildings on the site, allow the building to blend into its urban sur-roundings. In accordance with historical preservation regulations, the façade materials and building proportions have been newly interpreted with modern, light and transpar-ent structural components. The versatile symbiosis of colors, material and light gives the building its authenticity.

PROJECT FACTS

Address: Langenbeckstraße 1, 55131 Mainz, Germany. **Client:** LBB Niederlassung Mainz. **Completion:** 2008. **Gross floor area:** 52,000 m². **Main materials:** reinforced concrete skeleton structure, post and rail type façade, brick. **Building:** new construction. **Operator:** state.

↑ | **Information and access corridor**
↙ | **Ground floor plan,** with color guidance
system

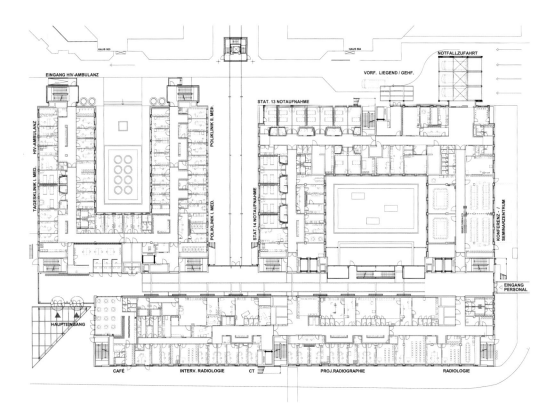

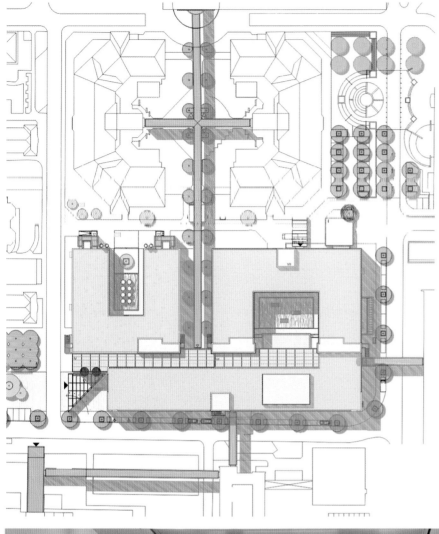

↖ | Site plan
↓ | Ward

↑ | **Detail,** façade
→ | **Façade,** facing courtyard

Extension Maxvorstadt Social Welfare Clinic

Munich

This private specialist inpatient clinic of the Diakoniewerk, located in Munich, specializes in caring for the elderly. The nursing areas have been extended and the entrance has been remodeled and improved. The new five-story building houses a two-story entrance lobby, opposite the new Pinakothek and gives the institution a stronger presence in the urban context. Geriatric and general care has been extended and modernized by 12 beds on each of the four floors. Particular attention was paid to providing interior spaces with ample daylight and comfortable treatment rooms. A terrace has been added to each of the levels. Four apartments for personnel have been added to the attic level. Space for public events and doctors' practices are located on the ground floor.

PROJECT FACTS

Address: Heßstraße 22, 80799 Munich, Germany. **Client:** Diakoniewerk München-Maxvorstadt. **Completion:** 2010. **Gross floor area:** 3,773 m². **Main materials:** natural stone façade. **Type:** general hospital. **Building:** new construction. **Treatment areas:** rehabilitation, physiotherapy. **Operator:** nonprofit.

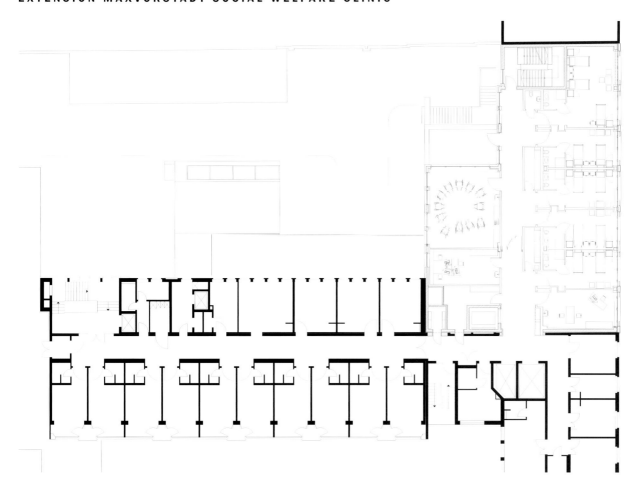

←← | **Façade,** facing street
↑ | **Second floor plan**
↓ | **Corridor,** ward

↑ | Main view
↗ | The "Why Green?" gallery
→ | Courtyard

Advocate Lutheran Hospital

Park Ridge

This patient care tower represents Advocate Lutheran General Hospital's commitment to patient-centered care with the addition of a significant building that improves the environment for patients, family and staff. Patient safety, floor plan efficiency, and improved quality-of-life for patients and caregivers drove the design. The new tower is the first LEED Gold hospital in Illinois and one of only a handful worldwide. Inpatient floors have been laid out in virtual "pods" using a universal floor plate design that can easily be converted based on future demand. Each pod has a decentralized nursing station to decrease noise levels and travel distances. The bed tower includes a public lobby/reception, pediatric units, an intermediate care unit, ICU and interventional unit, three 34-bed nursing units and a mother-baby unit.

PROJECT FACTS

Address: 1775 Dempster Street, Park Ridge, IL 60068, USA. **Landscape architect:** Andreas Brenner. **Client:** Advocate Lutheran General Hospital. **Completion:** 2009. **Gross floor area:** 38,500 m². **Main materials:** brick, Reynobond metal panels, hydrotech roof, grace air barrier. **Type:** adult and children hospital. **Building:** new construction. **Staff areas:** team centers throughout nursing unit. **Treatment areas:** pediatrics, surgery, oncology, mother and baby unit. **Operator:** private.

↑ | **Wishing well sink,** at pediatric unit entry
← | **Light-filled atrium**

← | Nurses' station
↓ | Ground floor plan

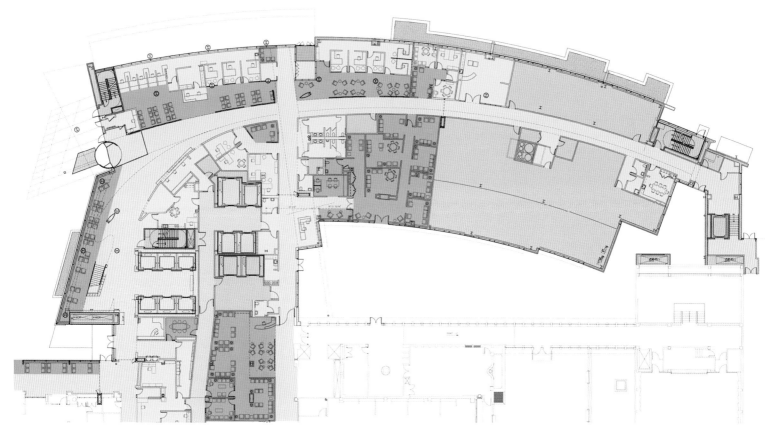

↑ | **North-east view,** Queens Hospital Center
↗ | **Interior corridor**
→ | **Lobby**

Queens Hospital Center – Ambulatory Care Pavilion

New York City

Perkins Eastman provided architectural and interior design for this ambulatory care facility that completes the replacement plan for this large public hospital. The new pavilion provides around 6,503 square meters of behavioral health, pediatrics, primary care, dialysis, dental, and eye care functions, as well as administrative, educational, and training facilities. The five-level building provides a signature landmark for the hospital campus and is linked to a new hospital building. The elegant building is organized by a 91-meter-long glazed public concourse along the southern perimeter. Composed of pre-cast concrete and a glass curtain wall, the building provides a light-filled two-story atrium, public entry plaza, and staff/service entry.

Address: 82–68 164th Street, New York City, NY 11432, USA. **Client:** New York City Health and Hospitals. **Completion:** 2006. **Gross floor area:** 1,340 m². **Main materials:** pre-cast concrete, glass, painted aluminum. **Type:** psychiatric, emergency medicine, pediatrics. **Building:** new construction. **Treatment areas:** operating rooms. **Operator:** state.

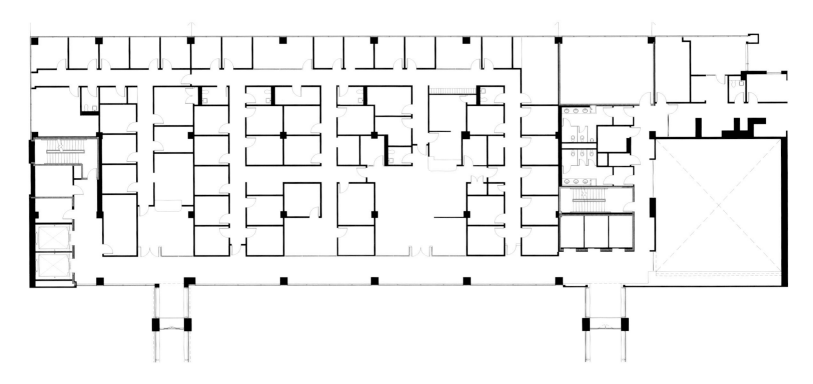

↑ | **First floor plan**
← | **Building front,** at dusk

← | **Building façade**, detail
↓ | **Second floor plan**

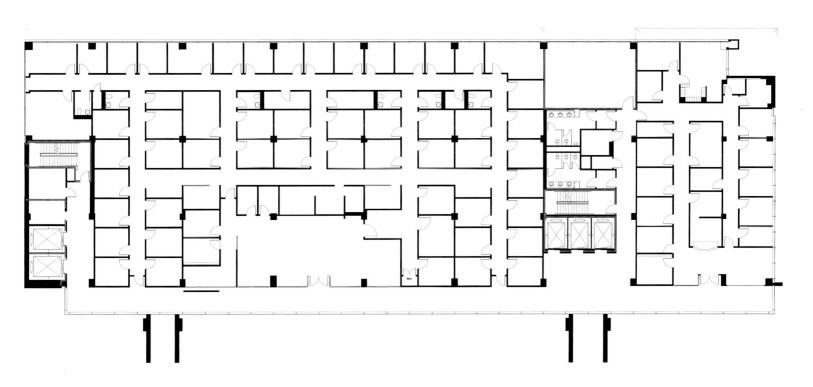

Swanke Hayden Connell
Architects

↑ | **King's Mill Hospital,** ward blocks
→ | **Internal street,** toward the main entrance

King's Mill Acute Care Hospital

Sutton-in Ashfield

The redevelopment of King's Mill Hospital was part of the Central Nottinghamshire Modernisation of Acute Services PFI (Private Finance Initiative) project by the Skanska Innisfree consortium. SHCA was the consortium's architect and design team leader for this 110,000-square meter new building and refurbishment project. The project is an extensive redevelopment of the existing acute facility to create a single unified hospital comprising a new state-of-the-art diagnostic and treatment center, a new emergency care and assessment center with an out-of-hours GP service, and a new, dedicated, women's and children's center. Three T-shaped ward buildings are linked together over five floors rising above the diagnostic, treatment and women's and children's centers. The 28 new wards, with around 50 % of the 654 new beds being in single rooms, predominantly enjoy a southerly aspect providing light and airy accommodation with views of the reservoir and countryside beyond.

Address: Mansfield Road, Sutton-in Ashfield, NG17 4JL, United Kingdom. **Client:** Sherwood Forest Hospitals NHS Foundation Trust. **Completion:** 2011. **Gross floor area:** 130,065 m². **Main materials:** concrete, polyester powder-coated aluminum curtain walling, glass, Sedum roofing. **Type:** emergency medicine, neo-natal, pediatrics. **Building:** new construction, renovation. **Treatment areas:** operation rooms, rehabilitation, water therapy, physiotherapy. **Operator:** public private partnership.

↑ | **Aerial view**
← | **Women's and children's center,** from
internal concourse

↑ | **Colored façade,** gives women's and children's center an eye-catching appearance
↓ | **Section**

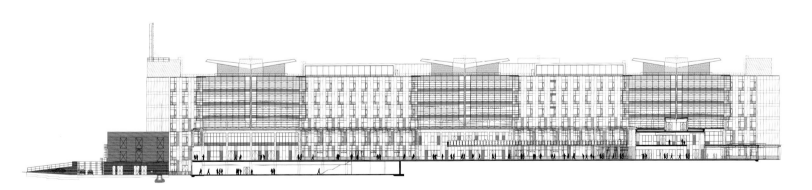

↑ | Adult area

Diabetic Center

Dubai

A key focus of the design for the new Dubai Diabetic Center (DDC) is to provide a welcoming environment for children that have to battle with illness every single day. The DDC has been designed with particular attention to separating flows, using gentle and curved shapes, bright and smooth colors, providing a comfortable environment with interactive play area complete with shelves full of toys and equipped with TV sets and games consoles. Wayfinding systems also use colors, so that the children can be sent to the "cyan room" instead of the "treatment room".

Address: Floor one, HH Sheikh Hamdan Bin Rashid Awards Complex, Plot 3210226, Madinat Dubai Al Melahe, Dubai, UAE. **Client:** Dubai Health Authority. **Completion:** 2012. **Gross floor area:** 2,000 m². **Type:** pediatrics, diabetes. **Building:** new construction. **Operator:** state.

↑ | **Pediatrics,** interactive play area
↓ | **Detail,** corridor

↓ | **Functional diagram**
↓↓ | **Floor plan**

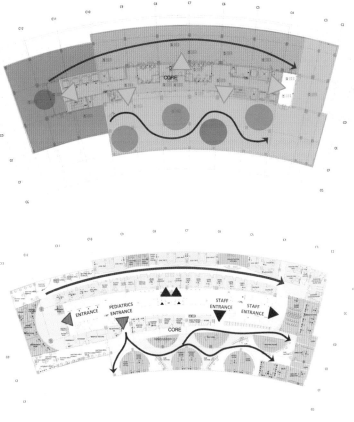

Rafael de La-Hoz

↑ | **Main view**
↗ | **Courtyard,** spaces for recovery
→ | **Patient room,** harmony and light

Hospital Rey Juan Carlos

Madrid

This new hospital is structured in three parallel buildings that reflect flexibility, expansion, functional clarity and horizontal circulations. The structure houses two hospital units. The gently curving oval crowns offer an interesting alternative to the more typical residential forms of the rationalist "block bar", and draw on the best of recent residential architecture: the elimination of corridors and annoying noise, concentric circulation. This architecture offers the professionals the opportunity to treat and the patients to be treated in an environment where the natural light and silence are conducive to a therapeutic atmosphere.

Address: Gladiolo Street, 28933, Móstoles, Madrid, Spain. **Client:** Madrilenian Public Health Service. Department of Health, Autonomous Community of Madrid. **Completion:** 2012. **Gross floor area:** 94,705 m². **Main materials:** aluminum, glass, concrete. **Type:** emergency medicine, ambulatory care. **Building:** new construction. **Treatment areas:** intensive care, operating rooms, consultation rooms. **Operator:** public private partnership.

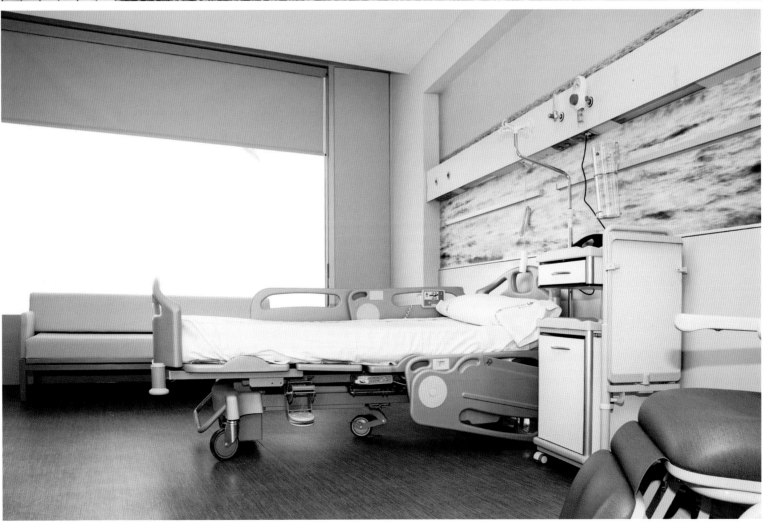

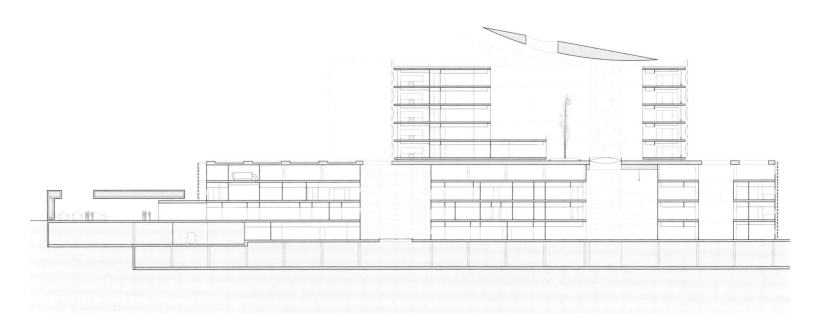

↑ | **Section**
← | **Emergency entrance,** functionality of building

↑ | **Hallway,** large base encompasses medical areas
↙ | **Axonometric**

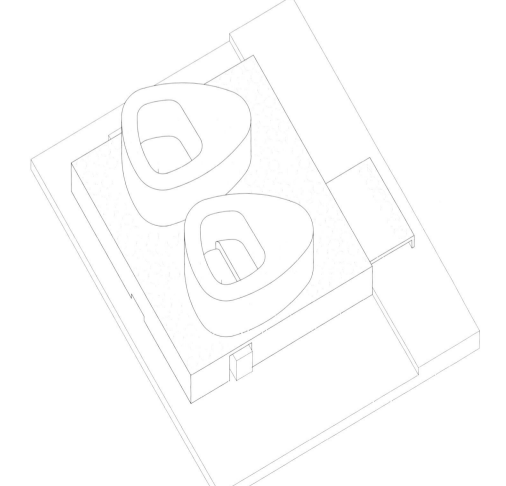

↑ | **Exterior,** with colorful façade panels
→ | **Main atrium,** sculpture by Alexander Knox

The Royal Children's Hospital

Parkville

The Royal Children's Hospital serves the community with 272 inpatient beds, 81 outpatient beds, and 30 emergency cubicles. Interactive playgrounds, two-story coral reef aquarium, meerkat enclosure, Scienceworks displays, and a stargazing starlight room are a few of the positive distractions for kids. More than 85 percent of the rooms are single-bed rooms, providing privacy for patients and their families. Rooms include state-of-the-art entertainment systems, access to lighting controls, a place to put personal belongings, and couches that convert into beds. Gathering areas and outdoor balconies are on each floor. A family resource center provides laundry areas, lounge, kitchen and an outside courtyard.

PROJECT FACTS

Address: 50 Flemington Road, Parkville 3052, Australia. **Client:** The Royal Children's Hospital. **Completion:** 2011. **Gross floor area:** 120,772 m². **Co-architects:** Billard Leece, Bates Smart. **Type:** pediatrics. **Building:** new construction. **Treatment areas:** operating rooms, rehabilitation, water therapy, physiotherapy. **Operator:** state.

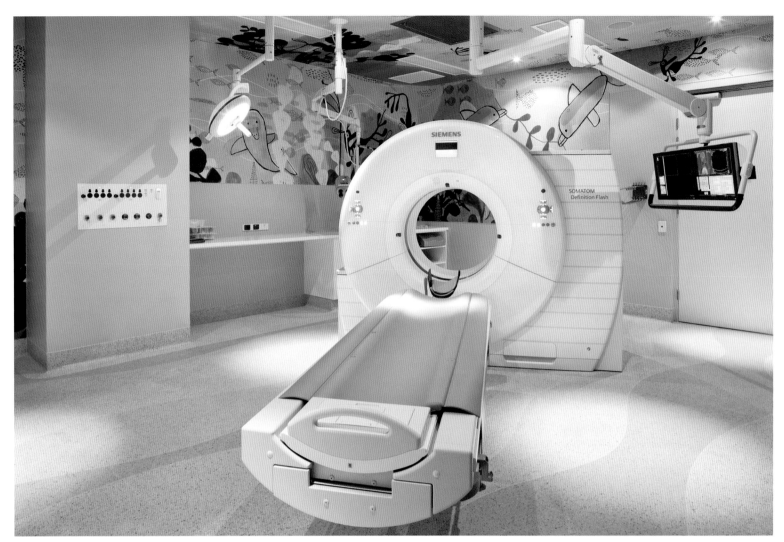

↑ | Imaging department
← | Ground floor plan

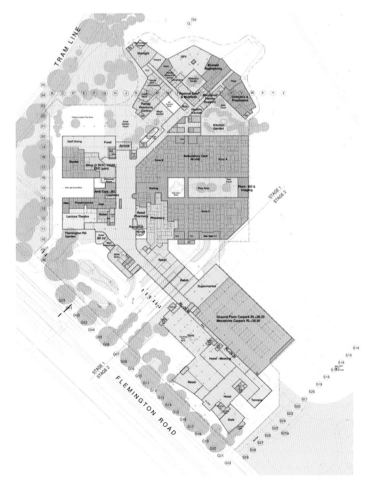

← | **Main lobby**
↓ | **Courtyard,** with meerkat enclosure

Nickl & Partner Architekten

↑ | **Entrance**, dialysis center
→ | **East façade**, evening

Dialysis Center Danube City

Vienna

As a clearly structured, welcoming building, this dialysis center in Vienna's Danube City offers a high-quality spatial experience. The new building comprises two circle segments and its main entrance opens out to the existing hospital building, located to the north of the new construction. A conference area, administration areas and supply rooms all join onto a large, brightly lit foyer. A total of 72 treatment areas with views of the surrounding greenery are spread across the two upper floors. A separate wayfinding system for patients creates a clear spatial arrangement. This system provides short routes and direct contact between nurses and patients.

PROJECT FACTS

Address: Kapellenweg 37, 1220 Vienna, Austria. **Client:** Wiener Dialysezentrum GmbH. **Completion:** 2009. **Gross floor area:** 6,254 m². **Structural engineers:** Rinderer & Partner ZT KEG, Graz. **Main materials:** post and rail type façade, wood, aluminum, sheet metal façade, sun shades. **Type:** dialysis. **Building:** new construction. **Operator:** private.

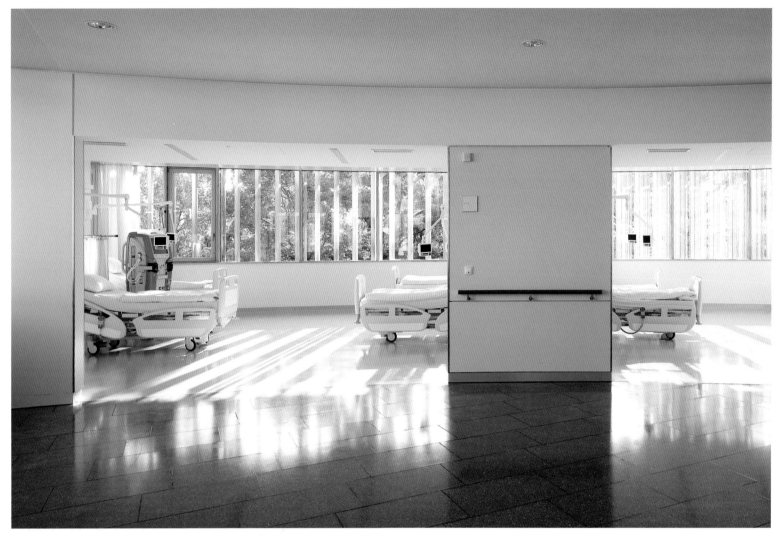

↑ | **Ward,** flooded with natural light
← | **Detail,** façade

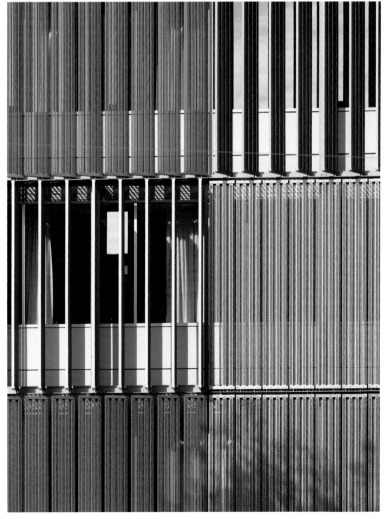

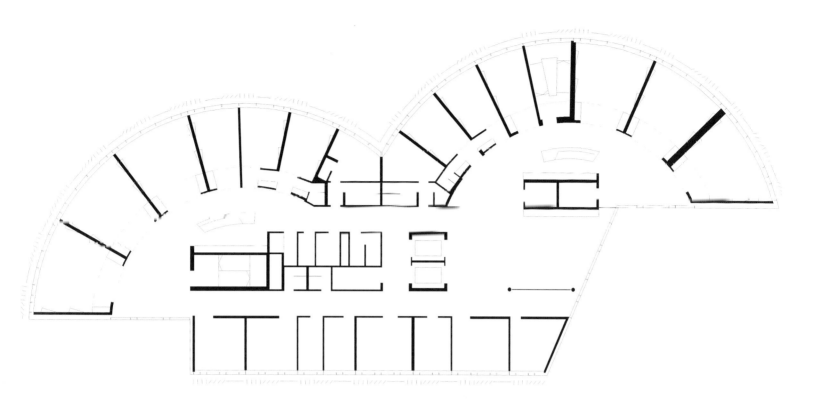

↑ | **First floor plan**
↓ | **View from west**, rear façade

Stefan Ludes Architekten

↑ | **Façade,** main entrance and new wing
↗ | **New lecture hall,** old brick building in background
→ | **Interior,** lecture hall

Mental Healthcare Department at Friedrich Schiller University

Jena

The main part of this hospital is a historical listed building, constructed by the architectural practice Gropius & Schmieden in 1879. Numerous structural and functional deficiencies lead to the decision for a complete refurbishment in 2002. Stefan Ludes Architekten developed a scheme that allowed them to maintain the historic structure, while simultaneously implementing facilities for today's medical demand. The carefully renovated buildings now house patient rooms and functional areas, while important secondary functions are located in the newly-constructed wings. A new lecture hall has been added to the east side. This has its own individual architectural expression and gives the campus a modern accent.

Address: Philosophenweg 3–5, 07743 Jena, Germany. **Client:** State of Thüringen represented by Staatsbauamt Gera. **Completion:** 2010. **Gross floor area:** 8,979 m². **Main materials:** ceramics, metal, brick work, aluminum, glass. **Type:** psychiatry. **Building:** new construction, renovation. **Operator:** state.

↑ | **Brightly lit modern lecture hall**
← | **Façade,** new wing at night

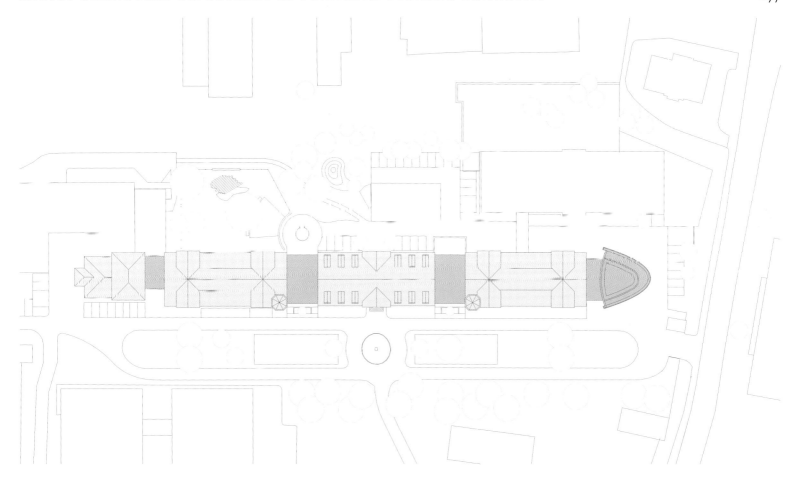

↑ | **Site plan**
↓ | **Lecture hall,** skylight

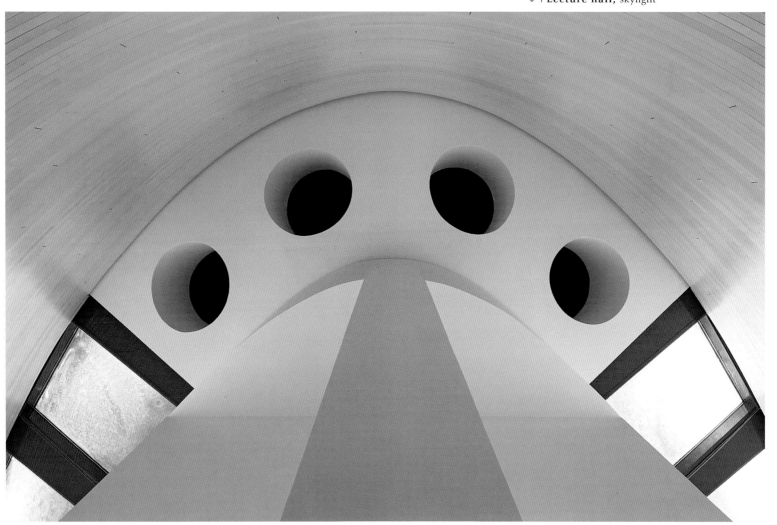

C. F. Møller Architects

↑ | **Distinctive building shape**, provides a
new landmark for the entire hospital complex
→ | **Interior courtyard**

Emergency and Infectious Diseases Unit

Malmø

The cylindrical Emergency and Infectious Diseases Unit at Malmø University Hospital is
designed to minimize the risk of spreading diseases. The distinctive shape also provides
a new landmark for the hospital complex. Patients enter the isolation ward via an airlock
from the walkway that surrounds the entire building. The exterior lifts are used exclusive-
ly by patients of the infectious diseases unit and for hospital waste, while the interior lifts
are used to transport staff, supplies and clean materials. Each story can be divided into
sealed-off smaller units in the event of an epidemic. C. F. Møller Architects furthermore
designed fixtures for the Emergency and Infectious Diseases Unit.

PROJECT FACTS

Address: Ruth Lundskogsgata 3, 20502 Malmø, Sweden. **Client:** Regionservice Södre Skåne. **Completion:** 2011. **Gross floor area:** 24,000 m². **Co-architects:** Samark arkitektur & design. **Artists:** Monika Gora, Jacob Dahlgren, Lena Ignestam, Mikael Johansson. **Main materials:** plastered and painted pre-cast concrete, glass. **Type:** infectious diseases unit. **Building:** new construction. **Staff areas:** staff room, canteen. **Operator:** state.

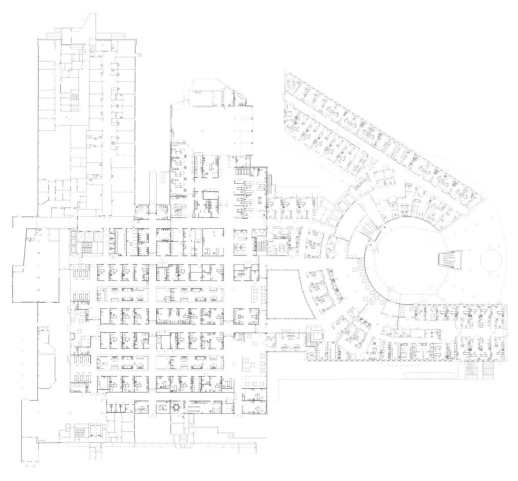

←← | **Façade**, detail
↖ | **Ground floor plan**
↓ | **Characteristic curved corridor**, repeating
colors of façade

↑ | **Main entrance**
→ | **Reception area,** with seating bench built
into reception counter

Particle Therapy Center

Marburg

This hospital offers treatment for cancer patients, as well as proton and heavy ion radiotherapy for outpatients. A special characteristic is the coordination between a linear
accelerator, a synchrotron, beam guidance and the individual rooms, where robots are
responsible for positioning patients in front of the ion beam. For the architects, keeping
these technical elements away from the view of patients was of paramount importance.
The side of the building where the main entrance is located is one large single opening.
This welcomes patients with a generous open gesture and masks the towering technical
building that rises behind it. Therapeutic needs and demands have resulted in a high
spatial density, a situation that has been resolved by the implementation of architectural
solutions that help to give the space a larger appearance.

PROJECT FACTS

Address: Baldinger Straße 1, 35043 Marburg, Germany. **Client:** Rhön-Klinikum AG. **Completion:** 2009. **Gross floor area:** 11,600 m². **Main materials:** exposed concrete, wodden post and rail façade, colored wall panels. **Type:** cancer. **Building:** new construction. **Treatment areas:** x-ray, radiation therapy, CT scanners. **Operator:** private.

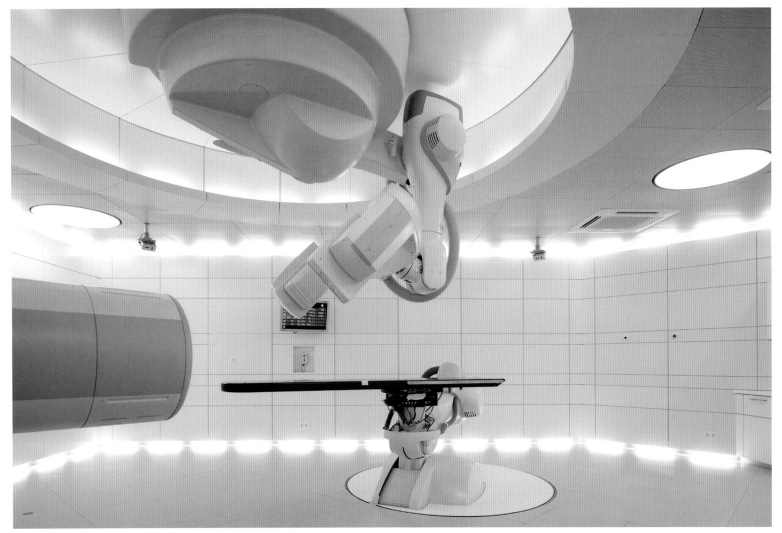

↑ | **Radiation therapy room**
↙ | **Site plan**

↖ | **Ground floor plan**
↓ | **Foyer,** reception desk and waiting area

↑ | **Massing,** two great rectangular volumes in concrete, fronted with glass, louvers and light shelves
→ | **Staircase,** bamboo on floors and steps

UCLA Outpatient Surgery and Medical Building

Santa Monica

Michael W. Folonis Architects have designed this healthcare center of the University of California, Los Angeles with a focus on patient experience and sustainability. The award-winning building – slated for LEED Gold certification – is an elegant balance of aesthetics, efficiency, and sensitivity. The massing of the building consists of two great rectangular volumes in a combination of board-formed and cast-in-place concrete, fronted with glass, louvers, and light shelves. The imperatives of transparency and function, and the aesthetic of early California Modernism, are all richly evident in the passive solar design, the building skin's glass and concrete, the interior's exposed steel, and sweeping sight lines both inside out and outside in.

Address: 1250 16th Street, Santa Monica, CA 90404, USA. **Client:** Sixteenth Street Medical Center LP. **Completion:** 2012. **Gross floor area:** 4,650 m². **Lighting designer:** Kaplan Gehring McCarroll Architectural Lighting. **Landscape architects:** Pamela Burton & Company. **Main materials:** cast-in-place concrete, glass, steel, bamboo. **Type:** cancer. **Building:** new construction. **Staff areas:** administrative offices, staff break rooms. **Treatment areas:** operating rooms. **Operator:** private.

↑ | **Building form is set back,** allowing a visitor friendly landscape
↓ | **Ground floor plan**

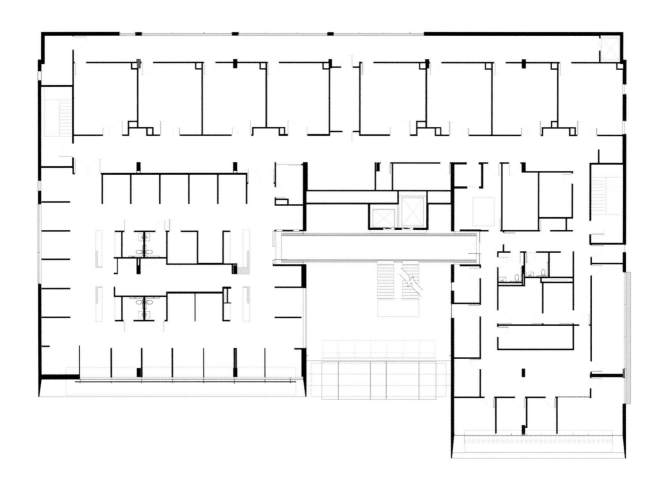

← | **Serious tone,** giving a solid form with physical lightness
↓ | **Ample expanses of bamboo,** adding elegance and a feeling of warmth

↑ | **Main staircase,** brightly lit by overhead skylights
↗ | **Perspective,** view from the north
→ | **Detail,** façade

Zentrum für Psychiatrie
Psychiatric Center Building

Friedrichshafen

This new building is embedded in the campus of the clinical center, on a gently sloping site next to picturesque orchards, oriented toward the Lake of Constance. The building is integrated into the sloping surroundings and consequently designed as a stepped hillside house, enclosing a generously-sized interior courtyard. A bridge frames the view of the hilly landscape, allowing one to feel the natural incline of the terrain even in the court-yard. The psychiatric center is visible from the landscape and provides spectacular views. A combination of exposed concrete and wood defines the surfaces of both the exterior and the interior. The vertically oriented cladding of untreated wood appears transparent and gives the building a light and open impression.

PROJECT FACTS **Address:** Röntgenstraße 8, 88048 Friedrichshafen, Germany. **Client:** Südwürttembergische Zentren für Psychiatrie Ravensburg. **Completion:** 2011. **Gross floor area:** 5,555 m². **Landscape architects:** Bernard und Sattler Landschaftsarchitekten, Berlin. **Main materials:** exposed concrete, wood. **Type:** psychiatry. **Building:** new construction. **Staff areas:** staff areas with kitchenette. **Treatment areas:** psychiatry, psychotherapy. **Operator:** state.

↑ | **Courtyard,** bridge connecting buildings
↓ | **Ground floor plan**

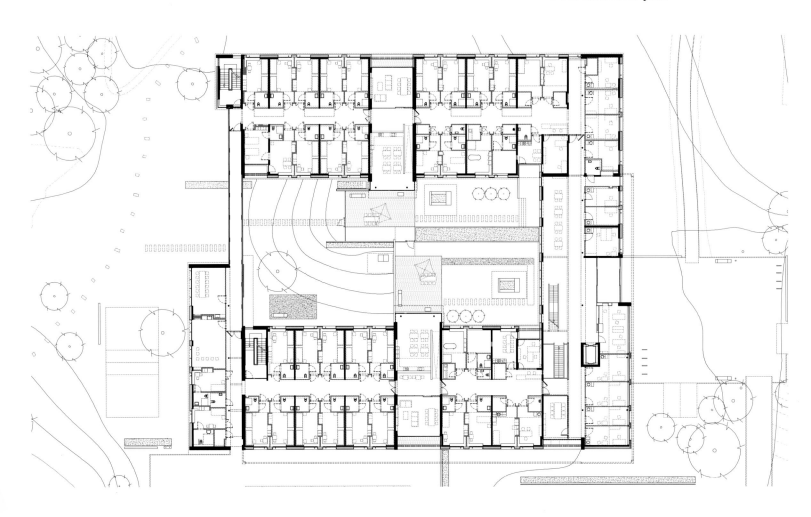

↖ | **Therapy room**
↓ | **Patient room**, bright and comfortable atmosphere

BP Architectures

↑ | **Stairwell,** adding a dynamic touch
→ | **Slender supports,** attaching structure

Stairwell Trousseau Hospital

Paris

The initial program involved the installation of three emergency staircases at Trousseau Children Hospital in Paris. This needed to be a functional object that would satisfy current regulations. The context of the project is an accumulation of architectural layers, which is typical of French public hospitals. The ensemble includes 19th-century buildings, a few additions from the 1970s that have more recently received new façades, a recent extension housing the maternity hospital and now three emergency staircases that needed to be fitted to the 1970s building within a short construction time frame. The eight-story structures add an element of surprise to the building ensemble and appear as a crinkled tower attached to the main building by means of slender supports.

PROJECT FACTS

Address: rue du Docteur Netter, 75012 Paris, France. **Client:** Hôpitaux de Paris – Hôpital Armand Trousseau. **Completion:** 2009. **Gross floor area:** 205 m². **Structural engineers:** Agence EVP. **Main materials:** iron, aluminum. **Type:** pediatrics. **Building:** new construction. **Operator:** state.

↑ | **Two of three emergency stairwells**
← | **Detail,** façade

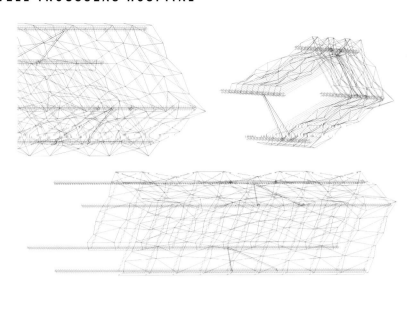

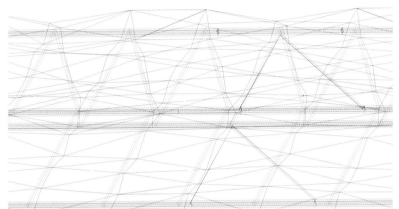

↖ | **Façade plan**
↓ | **Surrounding context,** includes many
different architectural elements

↑ | **Entrance corridor,** garden donor wall
→ | **Planetree family waiting room,** reception
and kitchenette

Neo-natal Intensive Care Unit

Danbury

Perkins Eastman completed a new state-of-the-art NICU for Danbury Hospital utilizing the Planetree patient care model. The new NICU offers the first single-room unit in
Connecticut comprising 15 single NICU patient rooms and four twin rooms, with trip-
let rooms available with adjoining single-room door access. Utilizing textures and colors
found in nature, the space creates a series of experiences for parents and staff and each
NICU patient room includes a dedicated family space. The design also focuses on a decentralized nursing approach providing a 1:1 or 1:2 nursing ratio depending on acuity of the
infant and direct views of and access to monitoring for each patient from these nursing
stations.

PROJECT FACTS

Address: 24 Hospital Avenue, Danbury, CT 06810, USA. **Client:** Danbury Hospital. **Completion:** 2011. **Gross floor area:** 1,670 m². **Main materials:** natural stone, graphic vinyl wallcovering, sculpted MDF wall panels, wood-patterned laminate, linoleum flooring. **Type:** neo-natal. **Building:** new construction. **Operator:** private, state. **Signage:** specific color palettes for each pod based on four elements of earth, fire, air, water.

↑ | **Entrance patient room,** decentralized nurses' station
← | **Graduates wall**

← | Family respite space
↓ | Second floor plan

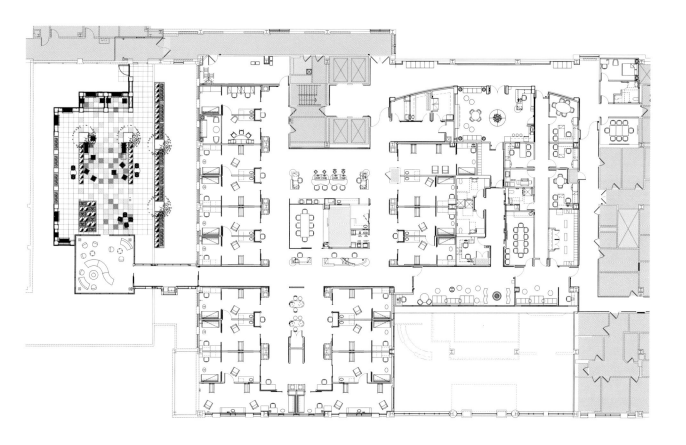

↑ | **Farewell room**
↗ | **Paintings,** on walls and floors
→ | **Information,** playing corridor

Princess Margaret Children's Hospital

Darmstadt

This 80-bed children's hospital is located on a park-like site in the grounds of Alice Hospital, on the outskirts of Mathildenhöhe in Darmstadt, Germany. The three-story building structure of the new ward has been inserted into the park and takes the abstract appearance of a large four-leafed flower. An advantage of this shape is the large curving façade surfaces, which allow maximum daylight into the all the rooms. Additionally, the cross-shaped circulation shortens the distances between the different areas for nurses and other personal. The patient rooms on the upper floors and housed in the outwards-projecting "flower petals" and open out in a trapeze shape. The funnel-shapped atrium in the center of the building allows light to flow into the interior.

PROJECT FACTS

Address: Stiftstraße 2, 64287 Darmstadt, Germany. **Client:** Stiftung Alicehospital. **Completion:** 2006. **Gross floor area:** 4,950 m². **Artist:** Holmer Schleyerbach. **Main materials:** end-grain wood, built-in cupboards wood veneer, epoxy resin. **Type:** pediatrics. **Building:** new construction. **Operator:** nonprofit. **Signage:** words and pictures.

↑ | **Patients' bathroom**
↙ | **First floor plan**

↑ | **Playing corridor,** patterned pillars
↓ | **Section**

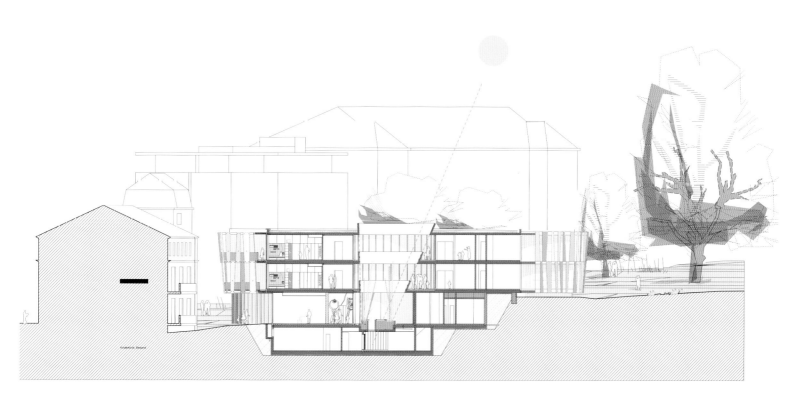

↑ | **Design concept,** creates tranquil and
relaxing space
↗ | **State-of-the-art patient room**
→ | **Noble anthracite,** with chrome accents

Sana Hospital

Bad Wildbad

The private station of the new Sana hospital building is characterized by its comfortably insulated and stress-free hotel atmosphere. The premier rooms are attractive for private patients who can enjoy hotel comfort in a warm atmosphere. Intelligent details and comfort elements are seamlessly integrated into the interior design. Alder surfaces and soft white nuances, together with the hygiene tested carpet, create a space for a high-stay experience, where patients experience a feeling of well-being. Anthracite in the bathroom reference the slate-clad bathrooms of upscale hotels. The high-quality materials complement the timeless elegance of the design.

Address: König-Karl-Straße 5, 75323 Bad Wildbad, Germany. **Client:** Sana Kliniken AG. **Completion:** 2009. **Gross floor area:** 8,700 m². **Main materials:** carpets, layered alder wood, glazed stone ware floortile. **Type:** general hospital. **Building:** new construction. **Operator:** private.

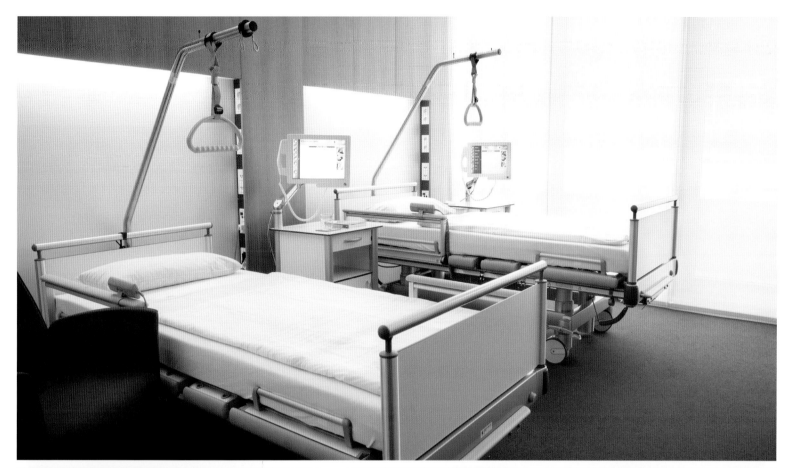

↑ | **Hotel atmosphere**
← | **Slate-inspired bathroom**

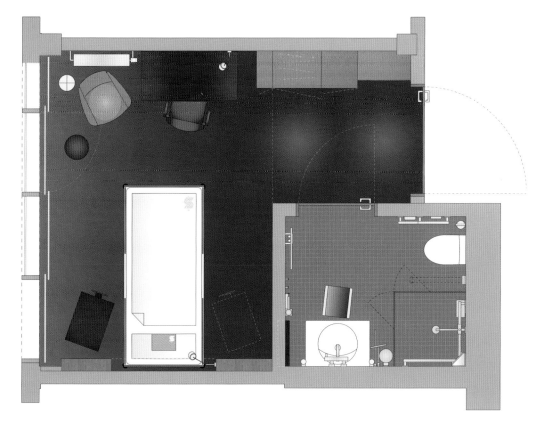

↖ | **Room layout**
↓ | **Room design,** comfortable understatement

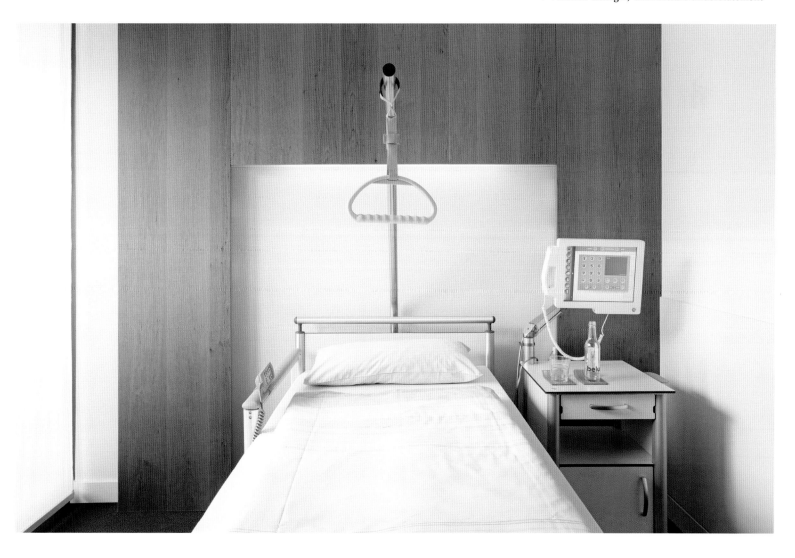

↑ | **West façade,** red cube houses treatment areas
↗ | **South façade**
→ | **Foyer,** case

Diagnostic and Neurological Care

Zschadraß

Originally designed as a pavilion system, this hospital in Zschadraß specializes in neurology and psychiatry and was built on the park-like site at the beginning of the 20th century. After extensive refurbishment work was undertaken on the existing buildings, the new building completes the ensemble and adds an urban accent to the site, situated between the neighboring building and residences to the north. The new structure is an appropriate addition to the historical ensemble. The wall panels of the north façade fold to form the horizontal roof surface and frames the entire structure. A red cube has been inserted under the roof and houses the treatment areas, operational units and administration offices. Amongst other things, the hospital houses a care ward, examination and treatment rooms of the two specialized departments.

Address: Im Park 15a, 04680 Zschadraß, Germany. **Client:** Diakoniewerk Zschadraß gGmbH. **Completion:** 2011. **Gross floor area:** 3,730 m². **Main materials:** reinforced concrete skeleton structure, post and rail type façade, Alucobond façade, greenery. **Type:** psychiatric. **Building:** new construction. **Treatment areas:** rehabilitation, water therapy, psyiotherapy. **Operator:** nonprofit.

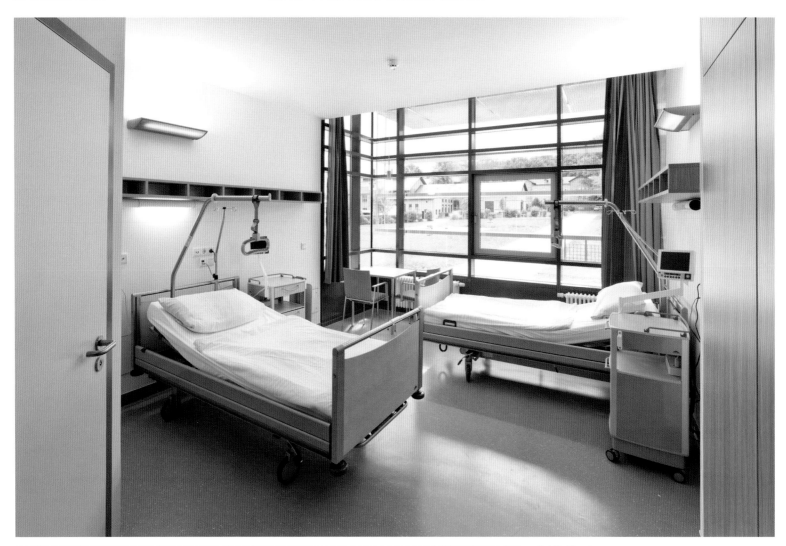

↑ | Patient room
← | Treatment room

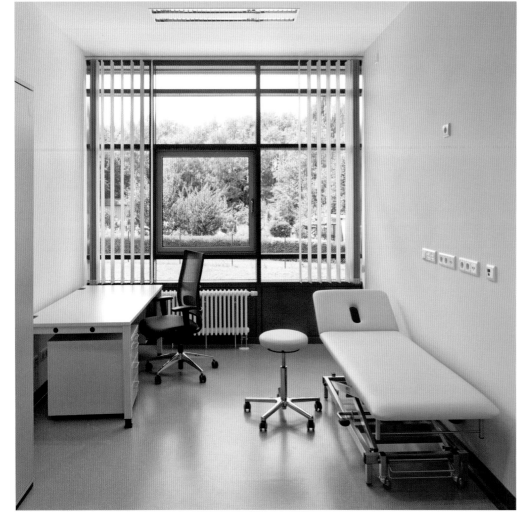

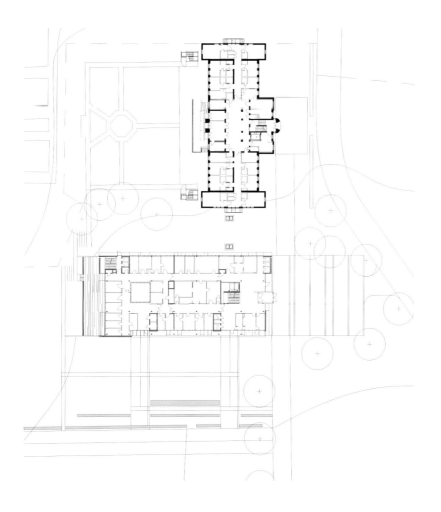

↖ | **Ground floor plan**
↓ | **East façade,** panels of the north façade fold to form horizontal roof

Schmucker und Partner
Planungsgesellschaft

↑ | **Main entrance**, artwork
↗ | **Main façade**
→ | **Patient suite**

Ethianum Hospital

Heidelberg

Ethianum Private Hospital in Heidelberg specializes in reconstructive and aesthetic plastic surgery, as well as preventative medicine. The clinic houses approximately 30 rooms with a maximum of 45 beds. Each room offers a balcony or loggia and the interior design takes its example from high-quality hotels. The complex, interdisciplinary technical solutions incorporated in the facility afford the building a high level of sustainability that is currently unique in Germany. The building is ventilated, heated and cooled by a zero-emissions geothermal energy system and at times of peak demand by a decentralized surface system. This reduces energy usage to an absolute minimum.

PROJECT FACTS

Address: Voßstraße 6, 69115 Heidelberg, Germany. **Client:** ILC Besitz GmbH + Co. KG, Heidelberg. **Completion:** 2010. **Gross floor area:** 11,000 m². **Interior design:** Gunther Spitzley AG, Kirchberg. **Main materials:** natural stone façade cladding, sandstone. **Type:** plastic surgery. **Building:** new construction. **Treatment areas:** operating rooms, physiotherapy. **Operator:** private.

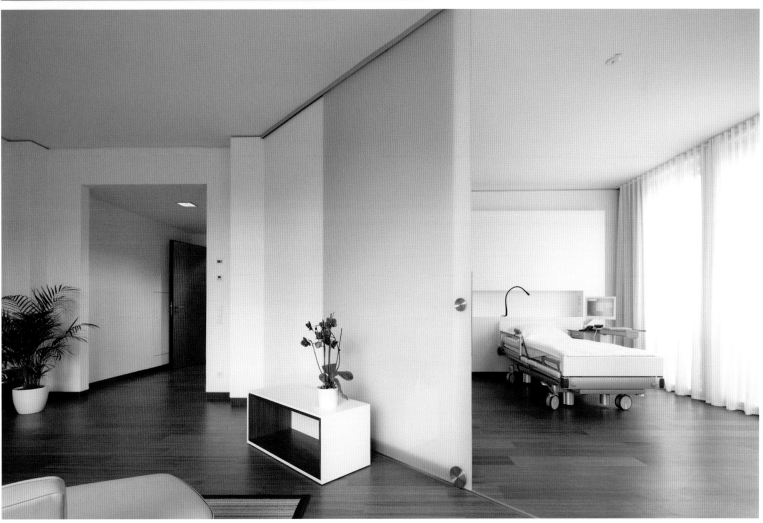

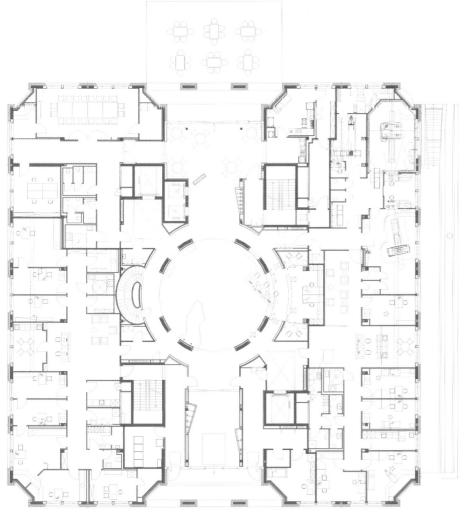

←← | **Rotunda,** with artwork
← | **Ground floor plan**
↓ | **Operating room**

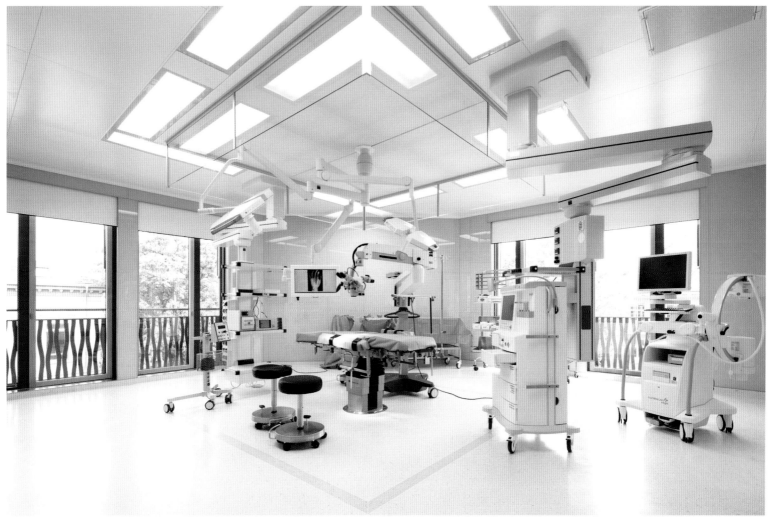

↑ | **South-west façade,** cantilevered building volume
↗ | **South-east façade,** with colored sun screen elements
→ | **Entrance area**

Forensic Psychiatry Building 17

Ansbach

The new psychiatry building number 17 provides forensic psychiatrists from Ansbach district hospital with a centralized building Had care ward. The new extension creates a nucleus for forensics and also incorporates sports therapy and occupational therapy. Strict security demands apply for the buildings 17, 18 and the planned building 16, which house preventative detention units and a psychiatric hospital. Despite these demands, the buildings have an open appearance with views of connections and links to the outside. A sensitive handling of space, material and light differentiates between open zones and private retreat areas. The architectural design provides an area that promotes therapeutic and re-socialization success.

PROJECT FACTS

Address: Feuchtwanger Straße 38, 91522 Ansbach, Germany. **Client:** Bezirk Mittelfranken. **Completion:** 2008. **Gross floor area:** 4,380 m². **Main materials:** reinforced concrete, flat roof, post and rail type façade, aluminum. **Type:** psychiatric. **Building:** new construction. **Treatment areas:** occupational therapy, sports therapy. **Operator:** state.

↑ | **Extension,** surprisingly open appearance
← | **Corridor,** floor-level windows establish a
relationship between interior and exterior

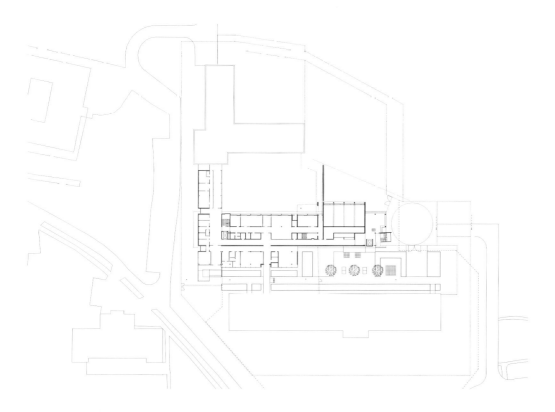

↖ | Ground floor plan
↓ | Recreation room

tönies + schroeter + jansen
freie architekten

↑ | **Entrance**
→ | **Entrance,** formed by rectangle inserted into building frame

Paracelsus Clinic

Osnabrück

The fusion of the radiotherapy clinic with the Paracelsus Clinic in Osnabrück has enabled the hospital to provide better care to cancer patients in Lower Saxony. Combining these two institutions has created a light-filled location that invites visitors to linger and relax. A cross-story frame characterizes the exterior appearance of the new building. This main structure is perforated by a slim rectangle and the combination of the two building components creates space for galleries, entrance areas and interior courtyards. One of Germany's most modern radiotherapy clinics, the open architectural style of this new building meets all the requirements associated with diagnostic, therapy and treatment in light and attractive spaces.

PROJECT FACTS

Address: Am Natruper Holz 69, 49076 Osnabrück, Germany. **Client:** Paracelsus-Kliniken Deutschland. **Completion:** 2008. **Gross floor area:** 17,309 m². **Landscape architects:** Freiraumplanung Uwe Gernemann, Bissendorf. **Interior design:** Ruge + Göllner Raumconcept. **Main materials:** reinforced concrete skeleton construction. **Type:** cancer. **Building:** new construction, renovation. **Operator:** private.

←←| **Inerior courtyard,** allows daylight to flow inside
↖ | **Ground floor plan**
↓ | **Waiting area**

↑ | **Pediatric wing,** from street
↘ | **Section**

Pediatric Wing

Póvoa de Varzim

The architects were awarded the contract to build a new pediatric wing on a very damaged 19th-century hospital. The idea was to create a building that doesn't look like a hospital, where children and adults could feel more comfortable. The simple, non-clinical, yet efficient space is dominated by a blue and white color code. The interior space is organized by two parallel corridors perforated by skylights that allow sunlight to stream into the space, creating a playful pattern of light and shade. The exterior attempts to resolve the volumetric relations with the preexisting building, creating a big frame that holds a dynamic white façade. The building is organized in a very free way in an attempt to open up the genre, making it more welcoming and accessible.

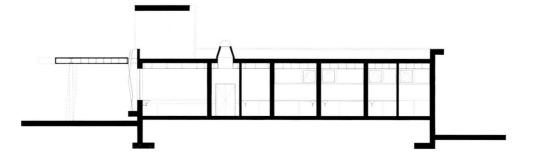

PROJECT FACTS

Address: Largo da Misericórdia, 4490-421 Póvoa de Varzim, Portugal. **Client:** Póvoa de Varzim and Vila do Conde's Hospital Center. **Completion:** 2008. **Gross floor area:** 330 m². **Main materials:** concrete, steel, perforated metal plate, aluminum, glass, vinyl flooring. **Type:** emergency. **Building:** new construction. **Operator:** state.

↑ | **Entrance canopy**
↓ | **Detail,** ceiling and lighting system

↑ | **Waiting area**
↓ | **Elevations**

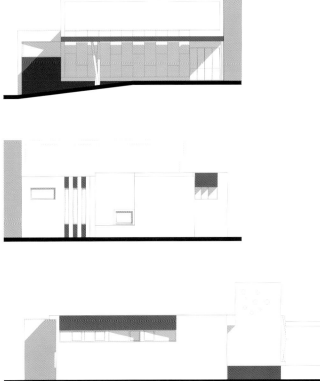

↑ | **Administration area**
→ | **Curved structure,** administration building
with care ward in the background

Mainkofen Hospital Receiving Station and Information Center

Deggendorf

This new construction houses the receiving station for the large psychiatric facility, and a forensic department. The existing listed Jugendstil buildings are of historical importance and particular care was taken in terms of situation, building height and choice of materials. Despite these considerations it was important to provide light-flooded attractive workstations and recreational areas. Many of the patients face a lengthy stay in hospital, so close attention was paid to the design of the patient accommodation and therapy rooms, as well as to the open areas.

Address: Mainkofen 6, 94469 Deggendorf, Germany. **Client:** Bezirk Niederbayern. **Completion:** 2006. **Gross floor area:** 3,706 m². **Main materials:** post and rail type façade with wood lamellae. **Type:** psychiatric. **Building:** new construction. **Operator:** state.

↖ | **Atrium,** allows lots of natural light inside
↑ | **Stairwell**
↓ | **Site plan**

← | **Administration,** landscaped surroundings
↓ | **Façade,** patient rooms

Sander Hofrichter
Architekten Partnerschaft

↑ | **Different wards,** have a villa-like appearance
↘ | **Section**

↗ | **Interior courtyard**
→ | **Detail,** façade

St. Josef Psychiatric Hospital

Neuss

This new structure completes the existing building of St. Josef Hospital in Neuss and provides a suitable environment for the mentally ill. The four three-story wards have the appearance of town houses and focus on providing patients with excellent living conditions. The clinic can accommodate 355 patients and offers only one- and two-bed rooms. The four wards all follow a clear design principle and create flexible care stations with up to 30 beds divided into two groups. The care support station is located at the ward entrance, providing an important control point; the communal and dining areas with kitchens and therapy zones are also located here. The atria in the buildings provide the corridors with adequate daylight and pleasant walkways for patients.

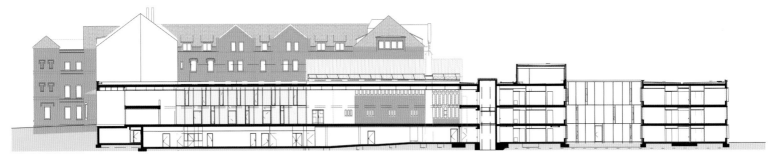

PROJECT FACTS

Address: Nordkanalallee 99, 41464 Neuss, Germany. **Client:** St. Augustinus Kliniken gGmbH. **Completion:** 2012. **Gross floor area:** 27,038 m². **Main materials:** exterior insulation finishing system (EIFS), casement windows. **Type:** psychiatry. **Building:** new building. **Staff areas:** cafeteria, tea kitchen. **Treatment areas:** physiotherapy, sports therapy. **Operator:** private. **Signage:** foliation on interior walls to aid orientation, color coding of individual houses.

↑ | Care support station
↙ | Ground floor plan

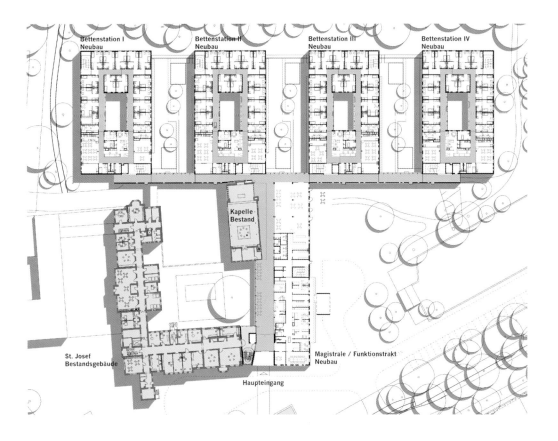

↑ | **Patient room**
↙ | **Site plan**

Jackson Architecture
McConnel Smith & Johnson
Architects

↑ | **Main building**
→ | **Façade,** allowing abundance of light inside

Olivia Newton John Cancer and Wellness Center

Heidelberg, VIC

The Olivia Newton John Cancer and Wellness Center is a holistically responsive design-solution to the varied and intricate facets of cancer care. The design is intended to support the role of family and friends and significantly emphasize patient experience and well-being. Pivotal to its design, the facility offers patients and staff continual access and visual connection to the central courtyard, which is gently wrapped and nurtured by the building façade. The design of the courtyard promotes wellness through restorative offerings of light, air, distraction and sustainability to both staff and patients of the facility – seamlessly connecting therapeutic and treatment environments with nature.

PROJECT FACTS

Address: 145 Studley Road, Heidelberg 3084, VIC, Australia. **Client:** Austin Health. **Completion:** 2012 (phase 1). **Gross floor area:** 25,000 m². **Main materials:** concrete structure, double glazing. **Type:** cancer. **Building:** new construction. **Treatment areas:** rehabilitation, physiotherapy. **Operator:** state. **Signage:** intuitive wayfinding organized around two circulation axes.

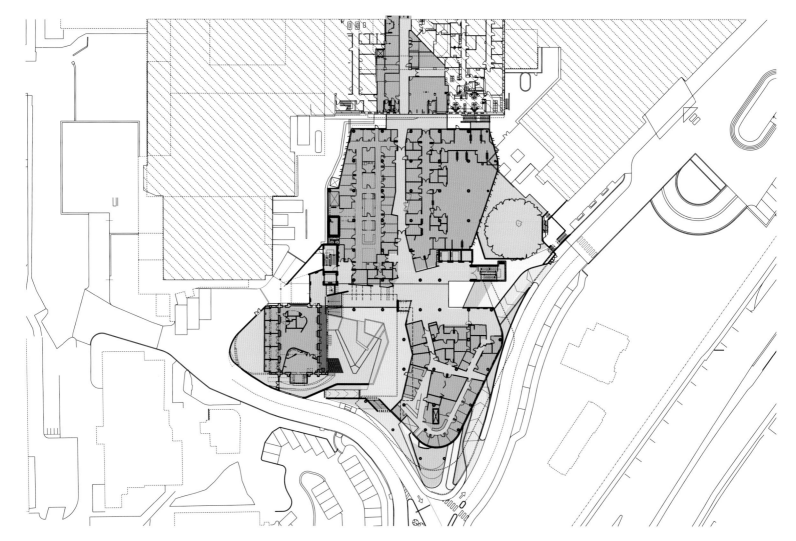

↑ | **Site plan**
← | **Atrium,** light-filled waiting area

← | **Modern interior design,** promoting patient well-being
↓ | **Detail,** façade

↑ | **Exterior,** local Arizona sandstone, plaster, and metal panels
↗ | **Natural building tones and materials,** inspired by surrounding nature
→ | **Large sweeping entry canopy,** protects patients as they enter

Peter and Paula Fasseas Cancer Clinic

Tucson

This cancer center by CO Architects invokes the power of the desert landscape to be defined as a place of inspiration and healing. The visual and physical access to Tucson's rugged natural outdoor beauty provides patients and staff with a connection to the healing power of nature. Three courtyards within the building bring abundant natural light to most spaces. Patients arriving at the clinic are protected from the elements by the large entry canopy and trellises that also provide shade to the interiors. The curved façade is welcoming as it literally and figuratively embraces patients, visitors, and staff. Interior finishes include natural materials such as stone flooring and wood paneling. The color palette is neutral earth tones.

Address: 3838 North Campbell Avenue, Tucson, AZ 85719, USA. **Client:** University Medical Center, University of Arizona. **Completion:** 2007. **Gross floor area:** 7,618 m². **Landscape architects:** Ten Eyck Landscape Architecture. **Main materials:** Arizona sandstone, plaster, metal panels, stone flooring, wood paneling. **Type:** cancer. **Building:** new construction. **Treatment areas:** rehabilitation. **Operator:** state.

↑ | **Three courtyards,** flood interior with
natural daylight
↙ | **Site plan**

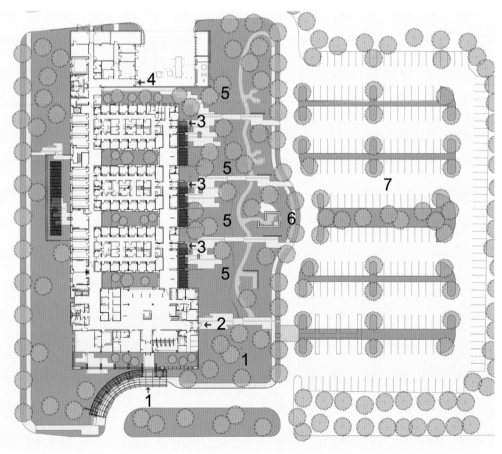

1. MAIN ENTRY
2. SECONDARY ENTRY
3. CLINIC ENTRIES
4. SERVICE ENTRY
5. HEALING GARDENS
6. MEDITATION GARDEN
7. PARKING

← | **Three clinic modules,** each designed around an outdoor courtyard
↓ | **Connecting bridge,** transports patients through landscape

↑ | **Main view**
↗ | **Main lobby,** information
→ | **Intensive care unit,** rooms

Center of Emergency Medicine in District Hospital

Kladno

This hospital project was based on the idea of concentrating all the demanding therapeutic and examination components into one area, thus forming the spine of the acute care hospital. New adequate spaces were also created that formed a pavilion of acute medical care. The design also intended that the new pavilion be integrated into the existing block. The inadequate transport connections to the city road network were also in need of an upgrade and the hospital building required new entrances with suitable dimensions to provide easy access for acute, emergency and immobile patients.

PROJECT FACTS

Address: District Hospital Kladno, Vancurova 1548, 272 59 Kladno, Czech Republic. **Client:** Central Bohemia Region, Czech republic. **Completion:** 2011. **Gross floor area:** 16,400 m². **Main materials:** reinforced concrete. **Type:** general hospital. **Building:** new construction. **Treatment areas:** operating rooms. **Operator:** state.

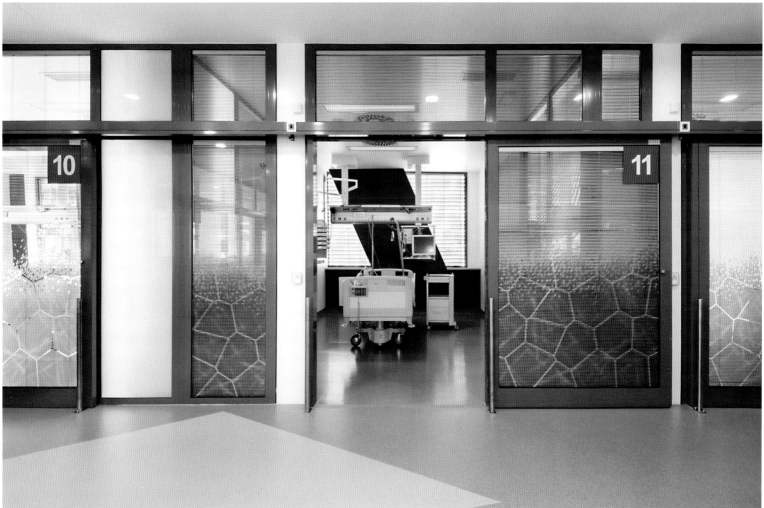

↑ | Waiting area
↓ | North-west façade

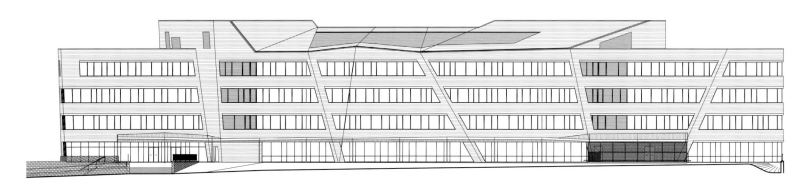

← | **Façade**, detail
↓ | **Third floor plan**

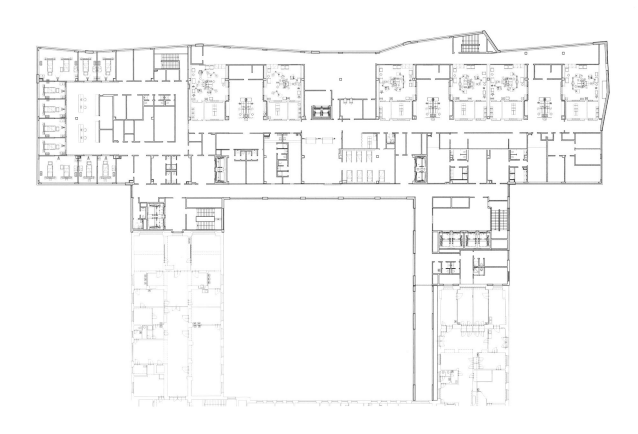

↑ | **Main view,** from street at dusk
↗ | **Main entrance,** recovery area
→ | **Lobby,** reception and hallway

Clinique Monet

Champigny

This hospital comprises four stories and a partial basement, situated in the center of the site along the north-south axis. It is set back approximately ten meters from the street, a design tactic that leaves space for an entry courtyard. The hospital houses 90 beds with ten additional beds for day patients. The rooms and living spaces are oriented east-west. The façades are clad in ribbed pre-enameled steel siding. The building is surrounded by green areas and ample parking space.

Address: Rue de Verdun, 94500 Champigny, France. **Client:** Générale de Santé. **Completion:** 2011. **Gross floor area:** 6,200 m². **Main materials:** concrete. **Type:** long-term rehabilitation, reeducation. **Building:** new construction. **Treatment areas:** physiotherapy. **Operator:** private.

↑ | **Lounge,** flooded with daylight
↓ | **Section**

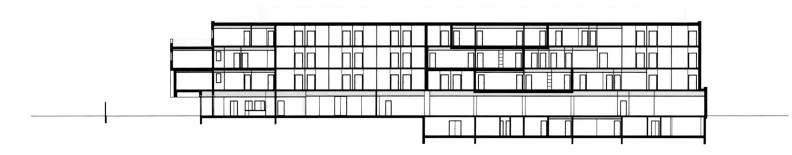

↑ | **Lobby,** exterior view
↓ | **Ground floor plan**

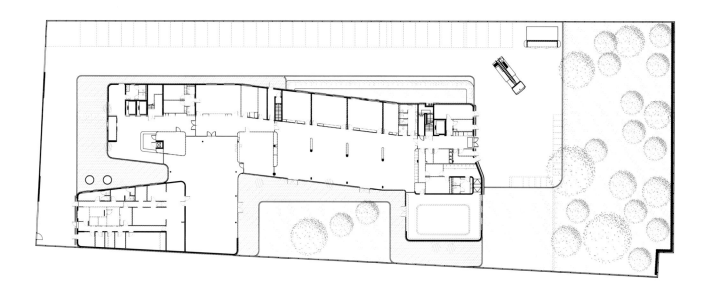

↑ | **Outpatient department,** landscape
designed as "pictures"
↗ | **Central park,** cheerful atmosphere
→ | **Children's yard,** important role of landscape

Hospital

Herlev

The extension of Herlev Hospital will comprise a new emergency department arcent and maternity services center, including a pediatrics unit and maternity ward. The winning project consists of three circular buildings placed on rectangular bases which are displaced from each other creating a number of inviting outdoor spaces. The new extension thus constitutes a down-scaled and compressed contrast to the 120 meter high rectangular geometry of the existing hospital. The recreational and healing effect of nature is well documented. At Herlev Hospital, this knowledge is taken seriously – thus, luxuriant courtyards, green roof gardens and a large, central green heart provide the new hospital with an altogether vibrant atmosphere.

PROJECT FACTS

Address: Herlev Ringvej 75, 2730 Herlev, Denmark. **Client:** The Capital Region of Denmark. **Completion:** 2017. **Gross floor area:** 52,000 m². **Landscaping architects:** SLA. **Main materials:** concrete, steel, glass, wood. **Type:** emergency medicine. **Building:** new construction. **Treatment areas:** operating rooms. **Operator:** state.

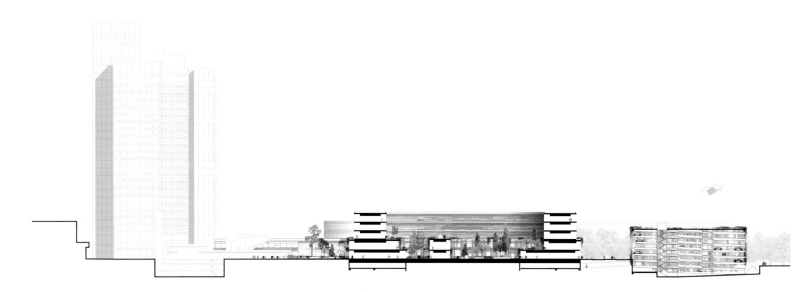

↑ | **Model**
← | **Bird's-eye view,** model

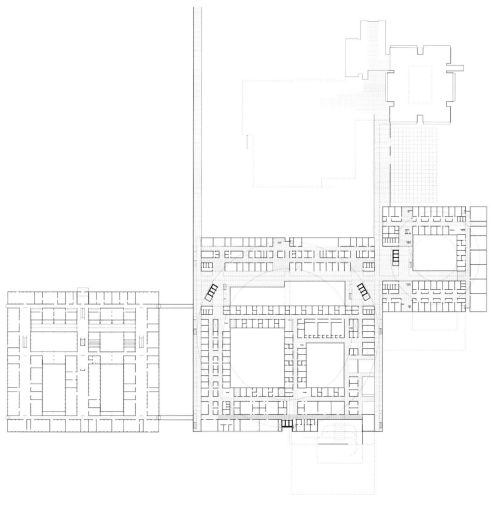

↖ | First floor plan
↓ | Main entrance

↑ | Aerial view
↗ | Inner courtyard
→ | Communal space

Livsrum

Næstved

Livsrum was the prize-winning project in a competition to design a new cancer counseling center at Næstved hospital in Denmark. The center is designed as a cluster of seven small houses situated around two green outdoor spaces. Each house has its own specific function and together they form a coherent sequence of different spaces. They offer a wide range of different rooms for informal advice, therapy and interaction with a focus on the users' comfort and well-being. The alternating roof line and careful material selection creates a unique architectural expression that merges the qualities of the surrounding typologies of single family housing and health care facilities.

Address: Ringstedgade 71–73, 4700 Næstved, Denmark. **Client:** Fællesfonden, Kræftens Bekæmpelse. **Completion:** 2013. **Gross floor area:** 772 m². **Main materials:** timber frame, fiber concrete. **Type:** cancer. **Building:** new construction. **Staff areas:** communal kitchen, dining area, lounge. **Treatment areas:** wellness, gym, rehabilitation area. **Operator:** nonprofit.

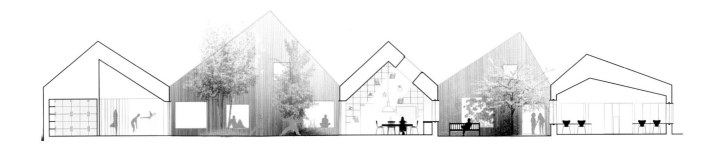

↑↑ | **Elevation**
↑ | **Section**
← | **View,** from street

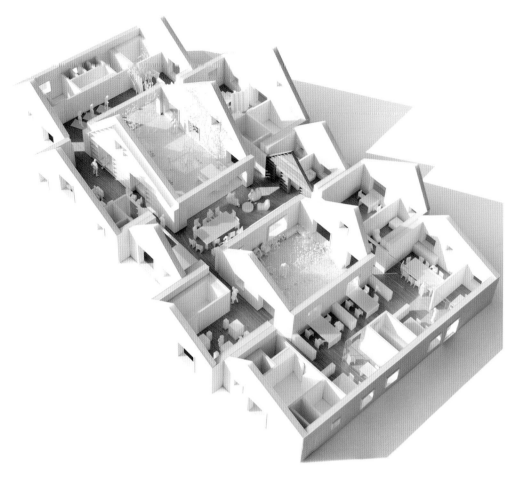

↖ | **Model,** bird's-eye view
↓ | **Garden,** view from window niche

↑ | **Foyer,** flooded with daylight
↗ | **Entrance hall,** evening view
→ | **Entrance,** access ramp

Evangelisches Waldkrankenhaus Outpatient Surgery Center

Berlin

This state-of-the-art surgical center is located in the grounds of the Waldkrankenhaus protestant hospital and is the result of remodeling work carried out on a simple building from the 1970s. The renovated building was designed to accommodate changes in the health care system and to relieve pressure on the existing classical surgery zone. The plans also ensure that the hospital remains sustainable in the future regardless of changes in medical techniques and treatments. The ambulatory surgical center houses two complete operating rooms and a procedure room, which can also serve as a third operating room if necessary. Openings in the ceiling in both the entrance hall and the preparation room create generous two-story spaces.

Address: Stadtrandstraße 555–561, 13589 Berlin, Germany. **Client:** Evangelisches Waldkrankenhaus Spandau Krankenhausbetriebs gGmbH. **Completion:** 2006. **Gross floor area:** 810 m². **Planning partners:** riedel architekten, Hamburg. **Main materials:** glass. **Type:** operating center. **Building:** renovation. **Treatment areas:** operating rooms. **Operator:** nonprofit.

↑ | **Perspective,** preparation room
↙ | **Site plan**

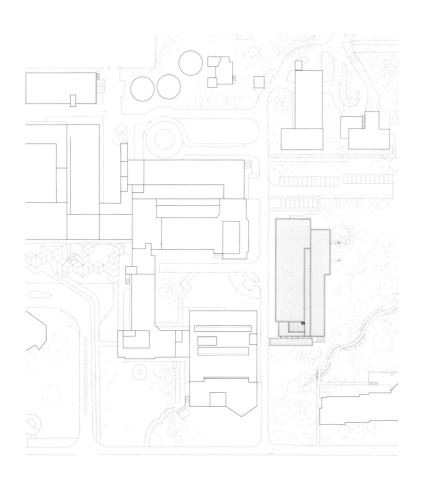

← | **Detail,** roof windows in foyer
↓ | **Passage,** connecting operating rooms

Feilden Clegg Bradley
Studios

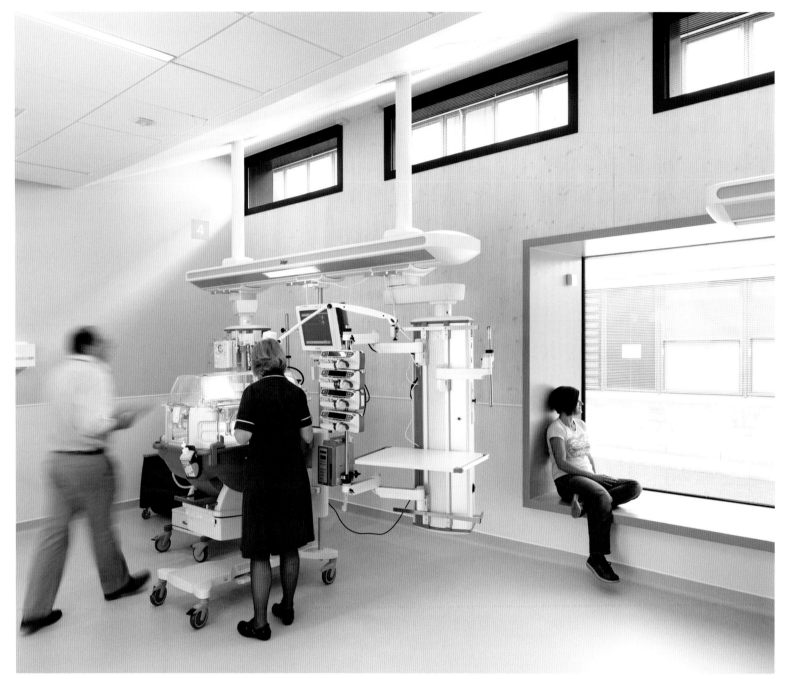

↑ | **Treatment facilties,** for premature and ill
babies
→ | **Large windows,** allowing natural light and
providing connections of interior and exterior

The Dyson Center for
Neo-natal Care

Bath

The Dyson Center for Neo-natal Care project has resulted in a dramatically different and
improved environment in which the Royal United Hospital can care for the 500 premature
and sick babies that it looks after each year. The feilding consists of a bingle-story new-build
extension, and the refurbishment of the space occupied by the previous NICU (Neo-natal
Intensive Care Unit) facility. The two elements are linked by a new "umbilicus", which provides an access point for emergency vehicles. The building zones define clear divisions for
infection control and access. The NICU provides the spaces with a visual connection with
the outside and minimizes reliance on artificial light. The timber solution used is a quick,
clean and a panelized form of construction, which also provided an opportunity to look at a
more sustainable material and creates a calm and stress-free environment.

PROJECT FACTS

Address: Combe Park, Bath BA1 3NG, United Kingdom. **Client:** Royal United Hospital, Bath. **Completion:** 2011. **Gross floor area:** 1,100 m². **Structural engineers:** Buro Hapold. **Main materials:** cross laminated timber. **Type:** neo-natal care. **Building:** new construction, renovation. **Treatment areas:** intensive care. **Operator:** state. **Signage:** colors on certain vertical surfaces further reinforce the legibility of the journey around the staff base from intensive care through to special care.

↑ | Interior courtyard
↓ | Sketch

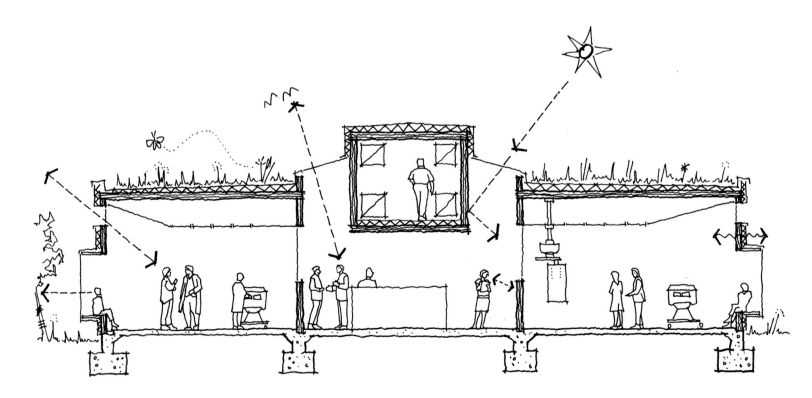

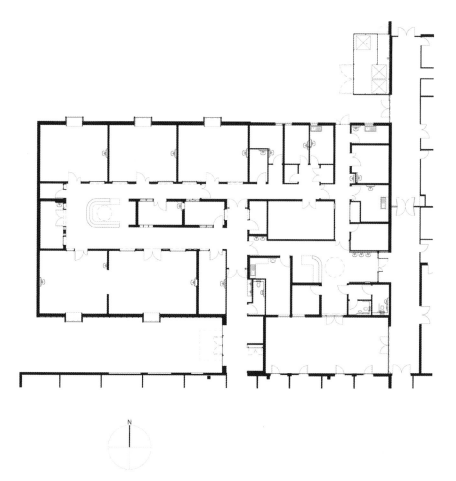

↖ | **Ground floor plan**
↓ | **Wayfinding systems,** reinforced by colors

↑ | **South-east façade,** technical passage
↗ | **Rear entrance,** via second floor
→ | **Corridor of consulting rooms,** with waiting area

Hospital-Residential Home

Granollers

This project involved the extension of the new outpatient buildings of Hospital Asil in Granollers, Barcelona, and its integration with the existing building. The original existing hospital was designed in 1910 and is listed as a historic building. The new building is defined by a rectangular volume that acts as a background to the original historical building. The general access is enhanced with a double-height hall and a large window that overlooks the city, allowing the existing building to be left unchanged. Moreover, two parallel volumes have been added to the main building complementing the outpatient facilities. The intervention also includes the reformation of the morgue, sterilization area, the laboratory, pharmacy, library and warehouse. The new façade has a neutral and homogeneous design, enhancing the historical value of the existing building.

PROJECT FACTS

Address: Avenue Francesc Ribas s/n, 08402 Granollers, Spain. **Client:** Fundación Francesc Ribas. **Completion:** 2009. **Gross floor area:** 19.570 m². **Structural engineers:** Manuel Arguijo. **Type:** emergency medicine. **Building:** new construction, renovation. **Treatment areas:** operating rooms, rehabilitation. **Operator:** private.

↑ | **Main hall,** connecting new and old building
↙ | **Second floor plan**

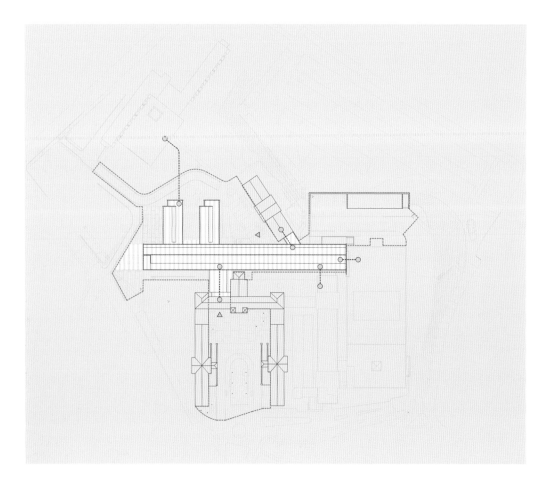

← | **Main hall,** with main entrance
↓ | **Entrance,** via second floor

↑ | **Main view,** restful surroundings
↗ | **Roof,** with interior courtyards
→ | **Foyer,** waiting area lit by atrium

Medical Care Center for Disabled Persons

Limay

This project engages in an equilibrium and disequilibrium between interior and exterior spaces, approaching both as materials. Contrary to programmed spaces, which are associated with specific functions, space pervaded by nature acquires a relaxing breath and a little freedom in defining its possible spaces. There are six internal courtyards situated within this four unit complex, which light the way along the paths toward the rooms. The passageway creates an efficient distribution of space. It alters according to the space it runs alongside; now rounded and harmonious, now straight and narrow. The palette of materials and colors also contains this diversity. Thus the space of the passageway is invigorated, becoming favorable to spontaneous action, to meetings and to sensory requests.

PROJECT FACTS

Address: 2 rue des Coquelicots, 78520 Limay, France. **Client:** SIEHVS + Sarry 78. **Completion:** 2012. **Gross floor area:** 2,560 m². **Main materials:** wood, plaster, stone. **Type:** medical care center. **Building:** new construction. **Treatment areas:** 55-bed residence with kitchen, dining facilities, gym. **Operator:** state.

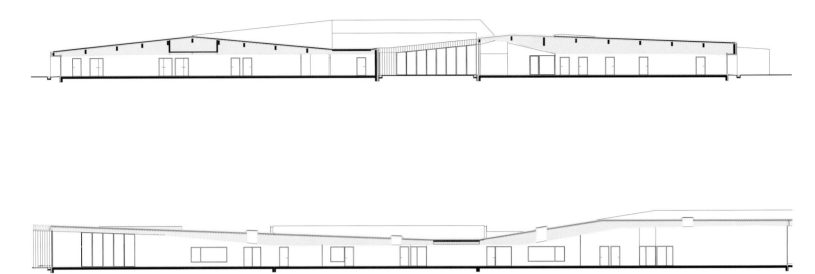

↑ | **Sections**
← | **Patient room,** red walls create warm
atmosphere

← | **Terrace,** view of surrounding street and landscape
↓ | **Ground floor plan**

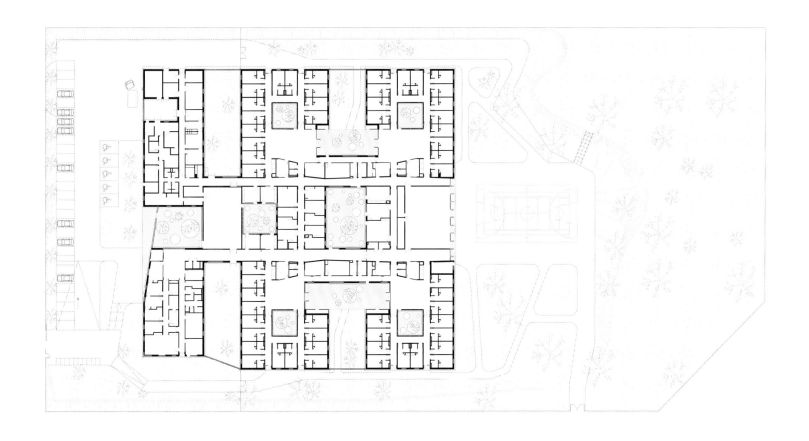

↑ | Main entrance
↗ | Labor delivery recovery room
→ | Lobby

North Shore LIJ Katz Women's Hospital and Zuckerberg Pavilion

New York City

The new Katz Women's Hospital building consolidates all women's medical services, provides spaces for the delivery of healthcare to expectant mothers, creates efficient medical linkages to the adjacent main hospital and acts as a new centerpiece for the revitalization of North Shore LIJ's (Long Island Jewish Health System) 19-hectare medical campus. This new building provides state-of-the-art facilities for diagnostic and treatment services, labor and delivery, antepartum and postpartum care, and includes 102 replacement beds and a nursery for 60 newborns. The hospital balances medical efficiency with comfortable patient and family-focused care and is compliant with the Green Guide for Health Care.

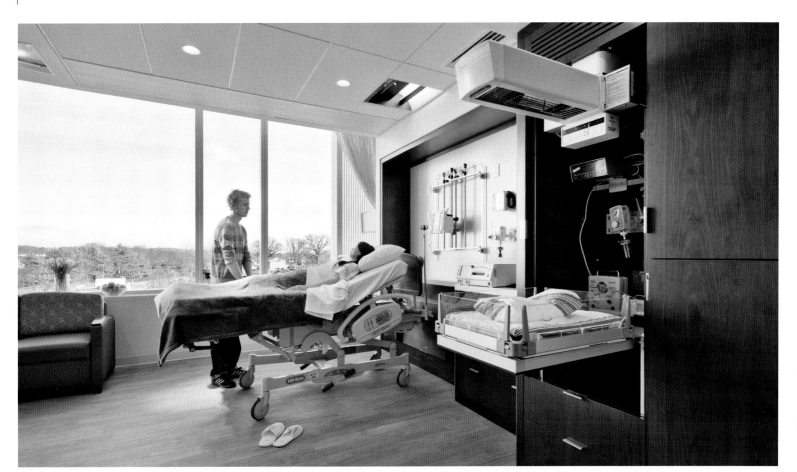

PROJECT FACTS

Address: 270-05 76th Avenue New Hyde Park, New York City, NY 11040, USA. **Client:** North Shore LIJ Health System. **Completion:** 2012. **Gross floor area:** 27,870 m². **Main materials:** curved glass façade, limestone base. **Type:** LDR (labor delivery and recovery). **Building:** new construction. **Treatment areas:** operating rooms. **Operator:** private.

↑ | **Main view,** at dusk
↓ | **Third floor plan**

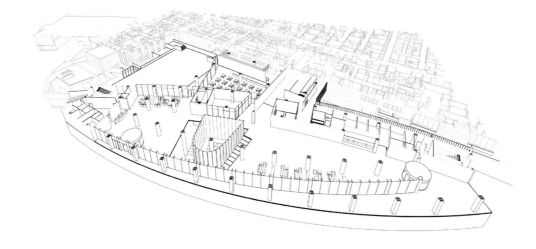

↖ | Building information model
↓ | Hallway curvature

↑ | Folded building volume
→ | Open interior coutyard

Lou Ruvo Center for Brain Health

Las Vegas

The Cleveland Clinic Lou Ruvo Center for Brain Health is located on a prominent "gateway" site in downtown Las Vegas. The center is intended to provide facilities that bridge all aspects of patient care, research, and education, which include an outpatient clinic, a research clinic, neuro-imaging suites, a reference library, community space and a multipurpose event/banquet center, as well as office space for Keep Memory Alive. The research facilities, clinical facilities, and offices are located within a four-story block that has been articulated as a series of offset rectangular shapes in white plaster and glass. The more public building uses are detached from the medical facilities across a dramatic covered trellis courtyard. These program functions are entered via an exterior breezeway through the medical office building. The Keep Memory Alive Event Center is contained within an expressive metal and glass form that is articulated as a curvilinear metal façade and roof with punched skylight openings.

Address: 888 West Bonneville Avenue, Las Vegas, NV 89106, USA. **Client:** Keep Memory Alive. **Completion:** 2009. **Gross floor area:** 6,225 m². **Planning partners:** WSP Cantor Seinuk, Cosentini Associates. **Main materials:** metal, glass, white plaster. **Type:** brain health. **Building:** new construction. **Treatment areas:** outpatient clinic, neuro-imaging suites. **Operator:** nonprofit.

↑ | **Office wing,** more rational and contained
↓ | **Section**

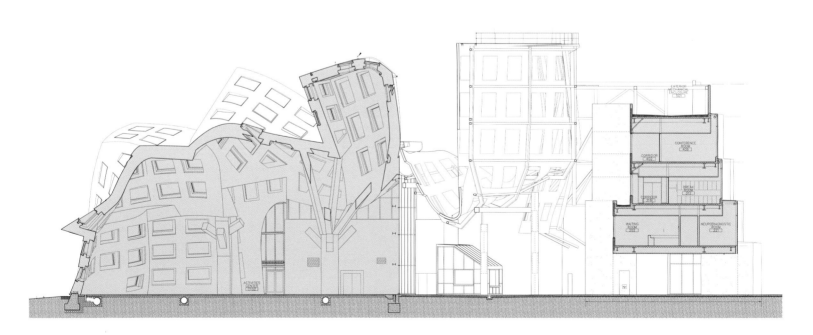

← | **Ceiling detail,** interior
↓ | **Foyer**

Rehabilitation Center Groot Klimmendaal

↑ | **Building,** shares a dialogue with surrounding forest
→ | **Seamless continuity,** between interior and exterior

Arnhem

In the undulating forest landscape around Arnhem Rehabilitation Center Groot Klimmendaal occupies a peaceful location hidden amongst the trees. The building has a small footprint and cantilevers over the surrounding terrain. Full height glazing along the central space connects the various internal elements kond ensures an valmost seamless continuity between interior and exterior. The energy usage is reduced by the compact building design and the design of the mechanical and electrical installations. Most notably the thermal storage contributes to the reduction of energy consumption. The design is the result of an intensive collaboration between architect Koen van Velsen and the users of the building. The customized design offers opportunities for different ways of using the building and the inevitable transformations of different departments within the client's organization.

Address: Heijenoordseweg 5, 6813 GG Arnhem, The Netherlands. **Client:** Stichting Arnhems revalidatiecentrum Groot Klimmendaal. **Completion:** 2010. **Gross floor area:** 14,000 m². **Structural engineers:** DHV Building and Industry BV, Rotterdam. **Type:** rehabilitation following illness, accident or birth defect. **Building:** new construction. **Operator:** nonprofit.

↑ | **Interior,** bright colorful space flooded with daylight
← | **Swimming pool**

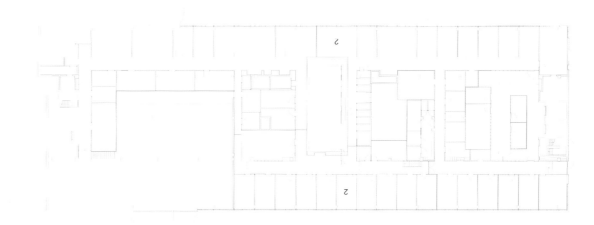

↑ | **Ground floor plan**
↓ | **Building volume,** cantilevered design
reduces building footprint

↑ | **Main view,** emergency entrance
↗ | **Heliport,** on roof
→ | **Intensive care unit**

Emergency Pavilion in Teaching Hospital

Hradec Králové

The orientation, architecture and functional layout of this hospital reflect the importance of the pavilion for emergency medicine. A related part of the construction is the landing area for helicopters: the body of which simultaneously creates a clear orientation point and dominant feature. As to its essence, the functional determination of the installation is not a very optimistic environment. Pain and sorrow are omnipresent. The architects' task and effort was to suppress and mitigate these feelings, at least as much as possible. The basic selected motif of graphic and color identification of the object is a meadow in blossom. The floral motifs permeate through the exterior and interior as a unifying line of the design in different technical and color types.

Address: Sokolská 581, 500 05 Hradec Králové, Czech Republic. **Client:** Teaching Hospital Hradec Králové. **Completion:** 2007. **Gross floor area:** 7,500 m². **Main materials:** reinforced concrete. **Type:** general hospital. **Building:** new construction. **Treatment areas:** emergency, crash room, intensive care. **Operator:** state.

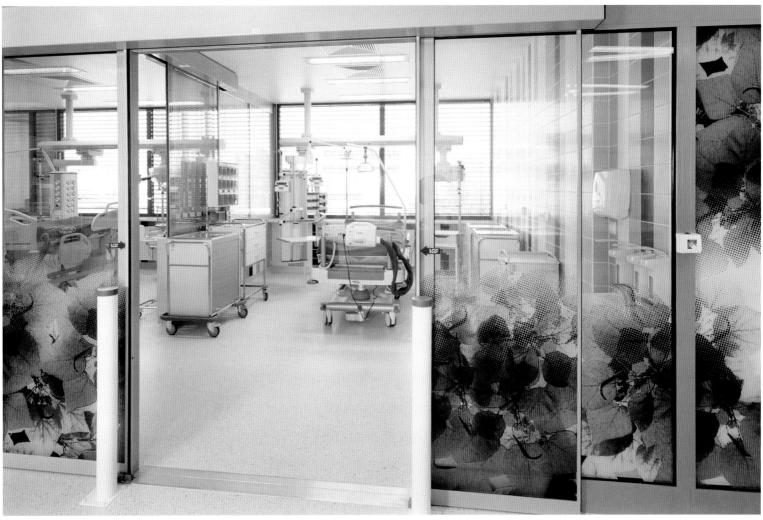

↑ | **Detail,** heliport
↓ | **Section**

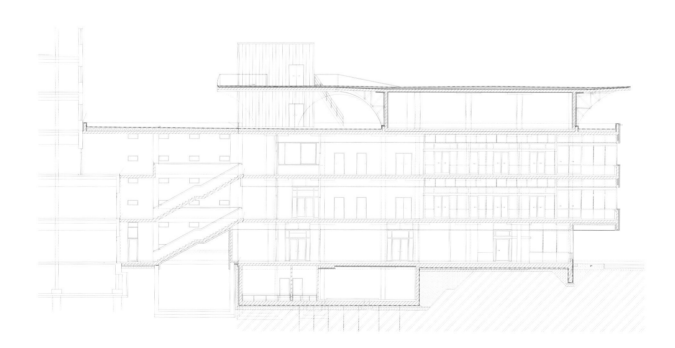

← | Waiting area
↓ | First floor plan

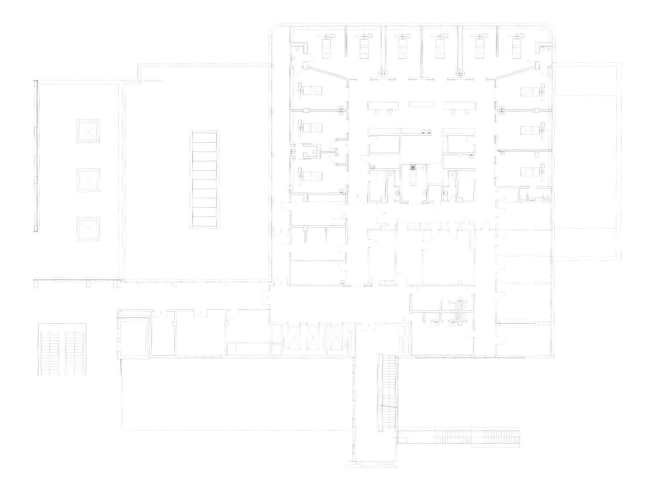

↑ | **Hallway,** window view
↗ | **Courtyard,** at night
→ | **Bird's-eye view,** site in winter

Psychiatric Hospital

Helsingør

The architects' research for Elsinore Psychiatric Hospital not only incorporated intensive analysis of the program and the needs of the clients, but also involved interviewing the daily users of the clinic: staff, patients and relatives. The different input from these interviews did not give any clear answers as to what the hospital should be like. Rather, they pointed out several paradoxes and ambiguities that the architects then brought into the project by transforming them into conflicting qualities of the program – to be and not to be a psychiatric hospital. A psychiatric hospital requires a clear, centralized functionality. At the same time it needs to look and feel like anything but a hospital. The snowflake structure lets all departments radiate in separate directions from a central node, leaving informal spaces within and around them. Also, it makes the hospital fold into the surrounding hilly landscape, disguising itself in order to optimize the cure of mental illness.

Address: Esrumvej 145, 3000 Helsingør, Denmark. **Client:** Frederiksborg County, Jette Sandberg. **Completion:** 2006. **Gross floor area:** 5,600 m². **Planning partners:** Julien De Smedt, NCC, Moe & Brodsgaard. **Main materials:** aluminum, glass, metal panels, pre-cast concrete panels. **Type:** psychiatric. **Building:** new construction. **Treatment areas:** communal areas, treatment rooms. **Operator:** state.

↖ | **Window niche,** in bright green
↑ | **Hallway,** foyer and waiting area in orange
← | **First floor plan**

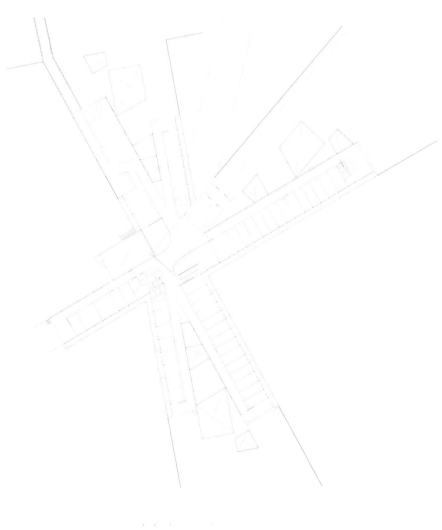

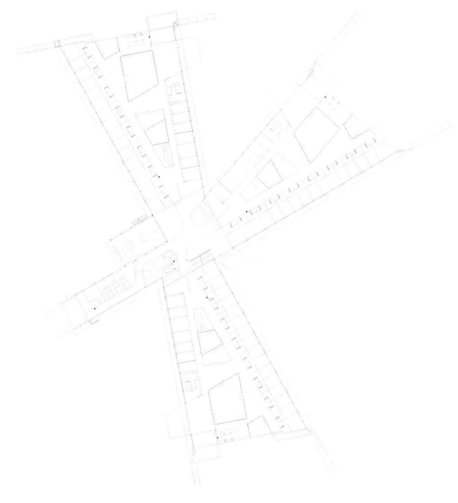

↖ | Second floor plan
↓ | Hallway

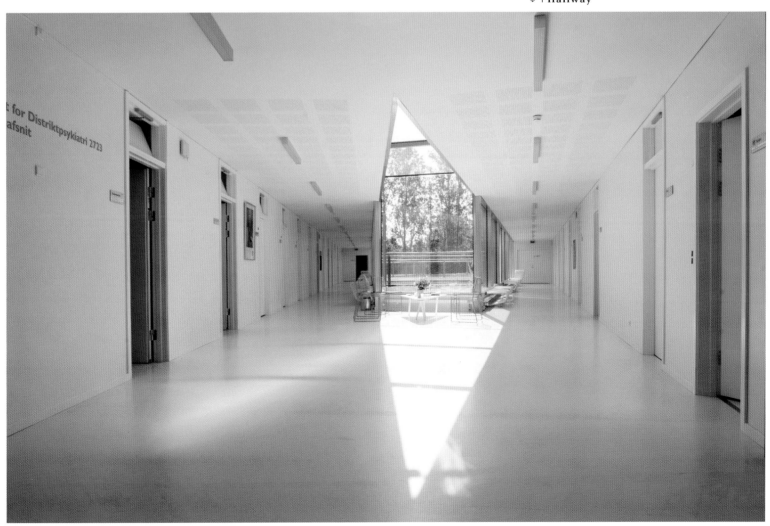

↑ | **Main façade,** from first building phase
→ | **Colorful façade,** complements green interior
courtyard

Children's Hospital

Shenyang

The design concept behind the Shenyang Children's Hospital was to allow the building to
tell its own lively story. Chinese signs of the Zodiac playfully decorate the façade, giving
it a lively appearance as it envelops the building with a delicate, shimmering gold veil. The
colorful nature of the façade and the green interior courtyards with recreation and play
areas create a welcoming, high-quality atmosphere. Great emphasis has been placed on
providing the hospitals with modern equipment and optimizing the operational processes
to meet the highest standards and current green-building concepts. Photovoltaic systems
and cooling ceilings that utilize ground water create a modern low-energy building.

Address: Chongshan Dong Road 74, Liaoning, Shenyang, Huanggu Qu, 110032 China. **Client:** Shenyang Children's Hospital. **Completion:** 2011 (phase 1). **Gross floor area:** 44,000 m². **Local general planner:** SADI – Shenyang Architecture Design Institute. **Main materials:** reinforced concrete, plaster façade, natural stone, metal screen, transparent ceiling. **Type:** pediatrics. **Building:** new construction. **Treatment areas:** operating rooms, rehabilitation, water therapy, physiotherapy. **Operator:** state.

↑ | **Façade,** Chinese Zodiac symbols
← | **Transparent ceiling,** allows daylight to flood inside

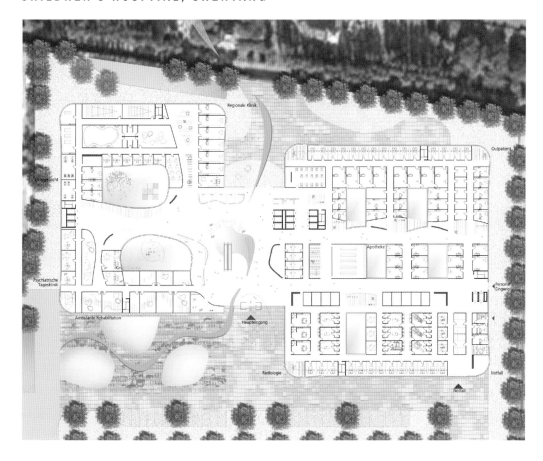

↖ | **Ground floor plan**
↓ | **View from interior courtyard,** cubes housing play areas

↑ | **Sculpturally folded roof,** offering a new interpretation of traditional architecture
→ | **Building volume,** designed to be open and welcoming

Maggie's Cancer Caring Center

Dundee

Maggie's Center Dundee is a small cancer patient care center located adjacent to the Ninewells Hospital on a site overlooking the Tay Estuary in Scotland. The center is intended to provide a calming environment in which newly diagnosed, recently relapsed, and terminally ill cancer patients and their family members can seek support and information on their illnesses. The building includes a small reception area, several offices and physical therapy rooms, a library, a terrace, and a kitchen in which visitors can relax or participate in group activities such as cooking lessons. Primary exterior materials include plaster, glass, and stainless steel panels, and the primary interior material is plywood.

Address: Ninewells Hospital, Tom McDonald Avenue, Dundee DD2 1NH, United Kingdom. **Client:** Maggie's Cancer Caring Centers. **Completion:** 2003. **Gross floor area:** 232 m². **Main materials:** plaster, glass, stainless steel panels, plywood. **Type:** cancer. **Building:** new construction. **Treatment areas:** consultation rooms. **Operator:** private.

↑ | **Tower,** reminiscent of traditional architecture
from the Scottish Highlands
↙ | **Sketch**

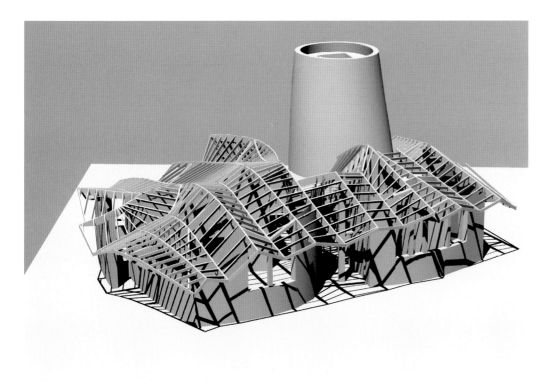

↖ | **Computer model**
↓ | **Reception and information areas**

↑ | **View north,** with George Washington Bridge
→ | **Atrium,** optimizes natural daylight inside
hospital building

Vivian and Seymour Milstein Family Heart Center

New York City

Set up high, this new heart center curves out toward an extraordinary landscape, acting as a counterpoint to the masonry buildings of the existing hospital complex that surrounds it. Waiting areas enjoy views of the Hudson River through frameless water-white glass and computer-controlled solar vanes, features of an innovative climate wall that admits a maximum of natural light while protecting the interior from excessive solar gain in summer and heat loss in winter. The transparency of the glass dissolves the barrier between the building's occupants and the exterior environment, while the material palette of the building – glass, stainless steel, aluminum, travertine – promotes a sense of lightness, clarity, and durability consonant with the process of healing.

PROJECT FACTS

Address: 177 Fort Washington Avenue, New York City, NY 10032, USA. **Client:** New York-Presbyterian Hospital/Columbia University Medical Center. **Completion:** 2010. **Gross floor area:** 11,613 m² (new building), 3,716 m² (renovation). **Associate architect:** daSilva Architects. **Main materials:** granite base and paving, glass climate wall with stainless steel support trusses, aluminum composite panels. **Type:** cardiology. **Building:** new construction, renovation. **Treatment areas:** operating rooms. **Operator:** private.

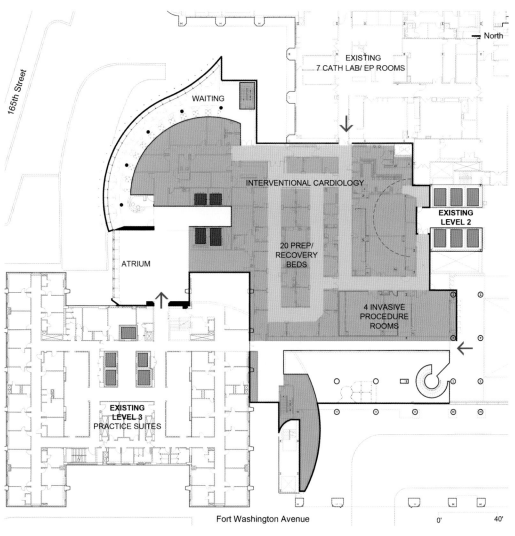

165th Street

North

EXISTING
7 CATH LAB/ EP ROOMS

WAITING

INTERVENTIONAL CARDIOLOGY

EXISTING
LEVEL 2

ATRIUM

20 PREP/
RECOVERY
BEDS

4 INVASIVE
PROCEDURE
ROOMS

EXISTING
LEVEL 3
PRACTICE SUITES

Fort Washington Avenue

0'   40'

←←| **Entrance**, 165th Street
↖ | **Second floor plan**
↓ | **Patient waiting area**

↑ | **Main view,** site
↗ | **Office suite**
→ | **Interaction space**

Memorial Sloan-Kettering Zuckerman Research Center

New York City

The new Memorial Sloan-Kettering Cancer Center (MSKCC) research building creates an inspiring, interactive and efficient environment for innovative cancer research, as well as a distinctive and distinguished civic identity for MSKCC, the world's oldest and largest private institution devoted to research, clinical care, and education in cancer. Located on a dense, urban site, the research building resolves MSKCC's persistent shortage of research space while responding to stringent urban design, zoning, and phasing constraints. At 23 stories tall, the new research building represents a new paradigm for urban research buildings.

Address: 415 East 68th Street, New York City, NY 10065, USA. **Client:** Memorial Sloan-Kettering Cancer Center. **Completion:** 2012. **Gross floor area:** 64,290 m². **Collaborating architect:** Zimmer Gunsul Frasca Architects. **Main materials:** fritted glass enclosure, open-jointed terracotta screen. **Type:** cancer. **Building:** new construction. **Operator:** private.

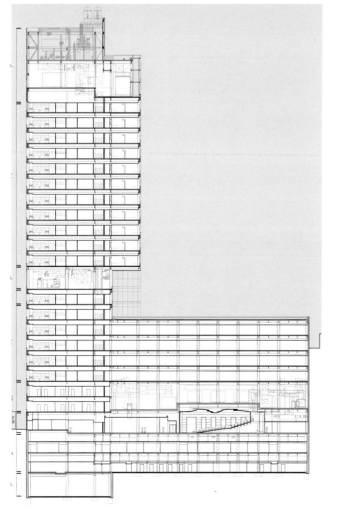

↑ | **North entrance**
← | **Section**

↑ | Laboratory
↙ | Typical floor plan

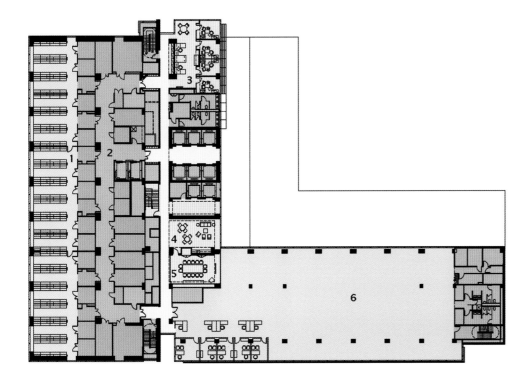

Index

Arch

A

Architects' Index

100% interior Sylvia Leydecker

Stammheimer Straße 113
50735 Cologne (Germany)
T +49.221.5708000
info@100interior.de
www.100interior.de

→ **306**

100 Planos Arquitectura
Eduardo Silva, Pedro Ferreira

Rua do Lidador 163
4480-791 Vila do Conde (Portugal)
T +351.252119372
info@100planos.com
www.100planos.com

→ **326**

3XN architects
Jan Ammundsen, Kasper Guldager Jørgensen,
Kim Herforth Nielsen and Bo Boje Larsen

Strandgade 73
1401 Copenhagen K (Denmark)
T +45.7026.2648
F +45.7026.2649
3xn@3xn.dk
www.3xn.dk

→ **206**

Studio Altieri SpA
Alberto Altieri, Giulio Altieri

via Colleoni 56/58
36016 Thiene (Italy)
T +39.0445.375300
F +39.0445.375375
info@studioaltieri.it
www.studioaltieri.it

→ **258**

Arcass Freie Architekten BDA
Otmar Müller, Bernhard Kullak, Erika Putz, Lucas Müller,
Manfred Ehrle

Urbanstraße 1
70182 Stuttgart (Germany)
T +49.711.238570
F +49.711.2385750
info@arcass.de
www.arcass.de

→ **166, 198, 218, 234**

Studio Asadov
Alexander Asadov

T +7.495.9366650
F +7.495.9366650
info@asadov.ru
www.asadov.ru

→ **154**

AZC Atelier Zündel Cristea
Irina Cristea, Grégoire Zündel

18 avenue Parmentier
75011 Paris (France)
T +33.1.55252494
F +33.1.43730282
agence@zundelcristea.com
www.zundelcristea.com

→ **348, 372**

BDP
Andrew Smith

1 North Bank
Sheffield S3 8JY (United Kingdom)
T +44.114.2731641
F +44.114.2289925
sheffield@bdp.com
www.bdp.com

→ **66**

BIG - Bjarke Ingels Group
Bjarke Ingels, Kai-Uwe Bergmann, Sheela Maini Søgaard,
Jakob Lange, Thomas Christoffersen, Andreas Klok
Pedersen, Finn Nørkjær, David Zahle

Nørrebrogade 66d, 2nd floor
2200 Copenhagen N (Denmark)
T +45.7221.7227
F +45.3512.7227
big@big.dk
www.big.dk

→ **392**

BP Architectures
Ignacio Prego, Jean Bocabeille

89 rue de Reuilly
75012 Paris (France)
T +33.1.53332420
F +33.1.53332421
agencebp@agencebp.com
www.agencebp.com

→ 294

Brullet Pineda Arquitectos
Manuel Brullet, Albert de Pineda

Travessera de Dalt 93–95 entsol. 1ª
08024 Barcelona (Spain)
T +34.932.106819
F +34.932.100214
pinearq@pinearq.com
www.pinearq.com

→ 100

Cannon Design

225 North Michigan Avenue
Chicago, IL 60601 (USA)
T +1.312.3329600
F +1.312.3329600
bonnen@cannondesign.com
www.cannondesign.com

→ 246

Casa Sólo Arquitectos SLP
Bernat Gato, Francesc Pernas, Roger Pernas

Passeig Cordelles 16, 3º2ª
08290 Cerdanyola del Vallès (Spain)
T +34.93.5946520
F +34.93.5946521
mail@casasolo.es
www.casasolo.es

→ 50, 86, 128

Clark/Kjos Architects
Glenn Kasman, Herb Giffin, David Frum, Tom Clark,
Mark Howell

333 NW 5th Avenue
Portland, OR 97209 (USA)
T +1.503.2244848
F +1.503.2247116
info@ckarch.com
www.ckarch.com

→ 38

CO Architects
Thomas W. Chessum, James S. Simeo

5055 Wilshire Boulevard 9th Floor
Los Angeles, CA 90036 (USA)
T +1.323.5250500
F +1.323.5250955
inquiries@coarchitects.com
www.coarchitects.com

→ 30, 340

Swanke Hayden Connell Architects

25 Christopher Street
London, EC2A 2BS (United Kingdon)
T +44.207.4548200
F +44.207.4548400
general@shca.com
www.shca.com

→ 254

Corea & Moran Arquitectura
Mario Corea, Lluís Moran

Grassot 10–12 Baixos
08025 Barcelona (Spain)
T +34.934.760732
F +34.934.760748
info@mariocorea.com
www.mariocorea.com

→ 226

Domy
Michal Juha, Jan Topinka

Politických veznu 19
110 00 Prague 1 (Czech Republic)
T +420.224.233730
F +420.222.245346
domy@domycz.com
www.domycz.com

→ 344, 388

Effekt
Tue Hesselberg Foged

Siljangade 4, 2. sal
2300 Copenhagen S (Denmark)
T +45.30.136697
mail@effekt.dk
www.effekt.dk

→ 356

Dietmar Feichtinger Architectes

11 rue des Vignoles
75020 Paris (France)
T +33.1.43711522
F +33.1.43706720
contact.paris@feichtingerarchitectes.com
www.feichtingerarchitectes.com

→ 96

Feilden Clegg Bradley Studios
Matt Vaudin

Bath Brewery, Toll Bridge Road
Bath BA1 7DE (United Kingdom)
T +44.1225.852545
F +44.1225.852528
bath@fcbstudios.com
www.fcbstudios.com

→ 364

Michael W. Folonis Architects

1424 Fourth Street, Third Floor
Santa Monica, CA 90401 (USA)
T +1.310.8993920
F +1.310.8993930
info@folonisarchitects.com
www.folonisarchitect.com

→ 286

Foster + Partners
Sir Norman Foster

22 Hester Road
London SW11 4AN (United Kingdom)
T +44.20.77380455
F +44.20.77381107
info@fosterandpartners.com
www.fosterandpartners.com

→ 18

FCP Fritsch, Chiari & Partner

Diesterweggasse 1
1140 Vienna (Austria)
T +43.1.90292
F +43.1.8946170
office@fcp.at
www.fcp.at

→ 96

Angela Fritsch Architekten BDA
Angela Fritsch

Auf dem Kreuzberg 1
64896 Seeheim-Jugenheim (Germany)
T +49.6257.648960
F +49.6257.6489699
info@af-architekten.de
www.af-architekten.de

→ 302

GBJ Architecture
Glenn Kasman, Herb Giffin, David Frum, Tom Clark,
Mark Howell

815 SW Second Avenue, Suite 600
Portland, Oregon 97204 (USA)
T +1.503.2230992
F +1.503.2943961
info@gbjarch.com
www.gbjarch.com

→ 38

Gehry Partners, LLP

12541 Beatrice Street
Los Angeles, CA 90066 (USA)
T +1.310.4823000
F +1.310.4823006
info@foga.com
www.foga.com

→ 380, 400

gpy arquitectos
Juan Antonio González Pérez, Urbano Yanes

Calle Castillo, 56, 2ºd
38003 Santa Cruz de Tenerife (Spain)
T +34.922.244575
F +34.922.151049
estudio@gpyarquitectos.com
www.gpyarquitectos.com

→ 82

Haid +Partner Architekten
Brigitte Helene Haid, Prof. Hans Peter Haid

Krelingstraße 33
90408 Nuremberg (Germany)
T +49.911.9355390
F +49.911.93553955
info@haid-architekten.de
www.haid-architekten.de

→ 46, 310, 318

hammeskrause architekten bda
Markus Hammes, Nils Krause

Krefelder Straße 32
70376 Stuttgart (Germany)
T +49.711.6017480
F +49.711.60174850
info@hammeskrause.de
www.hammeskrause.de

→ 282

Architekten Heinz-Mathoi-Streli

-> Architekt Karl Heinz
-> Architekt Dieter Mathoi
-> Architekt Jörg Streli

Architekt Karl Heinz

Arzlerstraße 156
6020 Innsbruck (Austria)
T +43.512.263129
F +43.664.4404415
office@architektur-heinz.at
www.architektur-heinz.at

Henning Larsen Architects
Jacob Kurek, Louis Becker, Henning Larsen, Lars Steffensen, Mette Kynne Frandsen, Peer Teglgaard Jeppesen

Vesterbrogade 76
1620 Copenhagen V (Denmark)
T +45.8233.3000
F +45.8233.3099
mail@henninglarsen.com
www.henninglarsen.com

HKS, Inc.
Amaya Tames, Ricardo Rondon, Dulce Torres, Bob Billingsley, Bob Billingsley, Doug Compton, Ron Billard, Steve Trevenar, Derrick Wheeler, Keith Davis, Sheree Proposch, Jo Campbell, Mark Mitchell, Ron Dennis

1919 McKinney Avenue
Dallas, TX 75201 (USA)
T +1.214.9695599
F +1.214.9693397

Stephan Höhne Gesellschaft von Architekten mbH

Caroline-von-Humboldt-Weg 38
10117 Berlin (Germany)
T +49.30.88723920
F +49.30.88723901
mail@stephan-hoehne-architekten.de
www.höhne-architekten.de

Hospital Technology
Torsten Meyer

Friedrichstraße 120
10117 Berlin (Germany)
T +49.30.400545600
F +49.30.400545624
info@hospitaltechnologie.com
www.hospitaltechnologie.de

HSP Hoppe Sommer Planungs GmbH
Marcus Zehle

Löwenstraße 100
70597 Stuttgart (Germany)
T +49.711.976540
F +49.711.9765432
info@hoppe-sommer-architekten.de
www.hoppe-sommer-architekten.de

huber staudt architekten bda, Gesellschaft von Architekten mbH
Joachim Staudt, Christian Huber

Keithstraße 2–4
10787 Berlin (Germany)
T +49.30.88001080
F +49.30.88001099
info@huberstaudtarchitekten.de
www.huberstaudtarchitekten.de

HWP Planungsgesellschaft mbH
Klaus Luig, Peter Bonfert

Rotenbergstraße 8
70190 Stuttgart (Germany)
T +49.711.16620
F +49.711.1662123
hwp@hwp-planung.de
www.hwp-planung.de

Jackson Architecture
Daryl Jackson, Alex Stephanou, Kathy Lakis, John Zadro

Level 2, 35 Little Bourke Street
3000 Melbourne (Australia)
T +61.39.6623022
F +61.39.6635239
info@jacksonarchitecture.com
www.jacksonarchitecture.com

Kasian
Wojciech Brus, John Etcher, Judith Horvath, Gus Spanos

155 West Pender Street, Suite 350
Vancouver, V6G 2T1 (Canada)
T +1.604.6384145
info@kasian.com
www.kasian.com

→ 202

Bettina Koenen

Falckensteinstraße 48
10997 Berlin (Germany)
T +49.30.21807379
office@koenenarchitektur.de
www.koenenarchitektur.de

→ 154

Richard Kroeker Design
Richard Kroeker, Brian Lilley

Piskwepaq Design, 2 Harbor Lane
West Pennant, Nova Scotia B3V 1M4 (Canada)
T +1.902.493277
richard.kroeker@dal.ca
www.richardkroekerdesign.com

→ 140

Rafael de La-Hoz Arquitectos

Paseo de la Castellana 82, 2ºA
28046 Madrid (Spain)
T +34.91.7453500
F +34.91.5617803
estudio@rafaeldelahoz.com
www.rafaeldelahoz.com

→ 260

Llewelyn Davies Yeang

Carlow House, Carlow Street
London NW1 7LH (United Kingdom)
T +44.20.76370181
F +44.20.76378740
info@ldavies.com
www.ldavies.com

→ 104

Stefan Ludes Architekten

Kurfürstendamm 177
10707 Berlin (Germany)
T +49.30.7001820
F +49.30.700182180
info@ludes-architekten.de
www.ludes-architekten.de

→ 190, 274

The Manser Practice Architects & Designers

107a Hammersmith Bridge Road
London W6 9DA (United Kingdom)
T +44.20.87414381
F +44.20.87412773
manser@manser.co.uk
www.manser.co.uk

→ 150

Architekt Dieter Mathoi

Meranerstraße 1
6020 Innsbruck (Austria)
T +43.512.580030
F +43.512.58003030
office@dmarchitekten.at
www.dmarchitekten.at

→ 162

McConnel Smith & Johnson Architecture

35 Richards Avenue
Surry Hills NSW 2010 (Australia)
T +612.8353.8888
F +612.9332.2402
www.msjgroup.com.au

→ 336

C. F. Møller Architects
Mads Mandrup Hansen, Klaus Toustrup, Mads Møller, Michael Kruse, Lone Wiggers, Julian Weyer, Klavs Hyttel, Anna Maria Indrio, Tom Danielsen

Europaplads 2, 11
8000 Aarhus (Denmark)
T +45.87.305300
cfmoller@cfmoller.com
www.cfmoller.com

→ 42, 92, 278

Müller & Klinger Architects Collective

Hohlweggasse 2/25
1030 Vienna (Austria)
T +43.1.5816280
F +43.1.58162820
office@ac.co.at
www.ac.co.at

→ 96

MVentrua & Partners, SGPS S.A.
Manuel Ventura

Rua Santos Pousada N.º 350, 4.º E 5.º Piso
4000-478 Porto (Portugal)
T +351.2.22086253
mv@mventura.com
www.mventura.com

→ 110

Nickl & Partner Architekten AG
Gerhard Eckl, Christine Nickl-Weller, Hans Nickl

Lindberghstraße 19
80939 Munich (Germany)
T +49.89.3605140
F +49.89.36051499
mail@nickl-partner.com
www.nickl-partner.com

→ 34, 146, 182, 270, 396

NSW Architects & Planners
Jon Arne Bjerknes, Marianne Hereid, Alfonso Rengifo,
Eli Undlien Søvik, Saba Naganathan, Søren Rehardt
Bech, Anders Alverfeldt, Johannes Eggen, Nora Kristine
Nordhaug, Anders Koller Tufte, Eva Grosen Husby, Anne
Røsstad, Lina Hyll, Erik Lind

P.O. Box 7057 Majorstuen
0306 Oslo (Norway)
T +47.22.930900
F +47.22.564160
nswap@nswap.no
www.nsw.no

→ 108

Jean Philippe Pargade

36 boulevard de la Bastille
75012 Paris (France)
T +33.1.43404100
F +33.1.43404500
contact@pargade.com
www.pargade.com

→ 90

Pei Cobb Freed & Partners LLP
Ian Bader

88 Pine Street
New York City, NY 10005 (USA)
T +1.212.7513122
F +1.212.8725443
pcf@pcf-p.com
www.pcf-p.com

→ 26, 136, 404

Perkins Eastman

115 Fifth Avenue
New York City, NY 10003 (USA)
T +1.212.3537200
F +1.212.3537676
info@perkinseastman.com
www.perkinseastman.com

→ 250, 298

Pich–Aguilera Architects
Teresa Batlle Pagés, Felipe Pich-Aguilera

Ávila, 138, 4r 1ª
08018 Barcelona (Spain)
T +34.93.3016457
F +34.93.4125223
info@picharchitects.com
www.picharchitects.com

→ 226

Pinearq S.L.U.P.
Albert de Pineda

Travessera de Dalt 93-95 entsol.1ª
08024 Barcelona (Spain)
T +34.932.106819
F +34.932.100214
pinearq@pinearq.com
www.pinearq.com

→ 368

Pitágoras Arquitectos
Alexandre Coelho Lima, Manuel Vilhena Roque,
Raúl Roque Figueiredo, Fernando Seara de Sá

Rua João Oliveira Salgado, 5c
4810-015 Guimarães (Portugal)
T +351.253.419523
F +351.253.518749
Pi.arquitectos@pitagoras.pt
www.pitagoras.pt

→ 132

Plischke Lühring Architekten GbR
Norbert Lühring, Armin Plischke

Am Viadukt 3–5
52066 Aachen (Germany)
T +49.241.701301-0
F +49.241.70130199
info@pl-architekten.de
www.pl-architekten.de

→ 186

Priebernig. 'P'

Wiesengasse 24
1090 Vienna (Austria)
T +43.1.3156902
F +43.1.315690350
heinz@priebernig.at
www.priebernig.at

→ 96

Atelier Thomas Pucher

Bahnhofgürtel 77/6
8020 Graz (Austria)
T +43.316.269378
F +43.316.26937828
info@thomaspucher.com
www.thomaspucher.com

→ 174

RDS Partner Architekten BDA
Peter M. H. Damm

Schleusenstraße 5
45525 Hattingen (Germany)
T +49.2324.92000
F +49.2324.920010
rdspartner@rdspartner.de
www.rdspartner.de

→ **210**

RRP architekten + ingenieure
Galuschka Fritz, Marc Rehle

Streitfeldstraße 37
81673 Munich (Germany)
T +49.89.9269070
F +49.89.92690732
rrp@rrp.de
www.rrp.de

→ **54, 170, 242, 328**

Sander Hofrichter Architekten Partnerschaft
Linus Hofrichter, Hubertus Sander

Kapellengasse 11
67071 Ludwigshafen (Germany)
T +49.621.586320
F +49.621.5863222
info@a-sh.de
www.a-sh.de

→ **78, 230, 332**

Schmucker und Partner Planungsgesellschaft
Andreas Schmucker

p3, 14
68161 Mannheim (Germany)
T +49. 621.107020
F +49.621.1070248
schmucker@schmucker-partner.de
www.schmucker-partner.de

→ **314**

SEED architects
Arnold Burger, Eduard Rothbauer, Guido Schuurman

Postbox 4050
8600 GB Sneek (The Netherlands)
T +31.72.5679010
info@seedarchitects.nl
www.seedarchitects.nl

→ **222**

SOM –
Skidmore, Owings & Merrill LLP

14 Wall Street
New York City, NY 10005 (USA)
T +1.212.2989300
somnewyork@som.com
www.som.com

→ **122, 376, 408**

Architekt Jörg Streli

Hinterwaldnerstraße 23
6020 Innsbruck (Austria)
T +43.512.280139
F +43.512.280139
architekt.streli@aon.at

→ **162**

TASH – Taller de Arquitectura
Antonio Sánchez-Horneros, Emilio Sánchez-Horneros

Calle La Granada 2
45001 Toledo (Spain)
T +34.925283430
F +34.925283431
tash@tash.es
www.tash.es

→ **114, 214**

TMK Architekten · Ingenieure
Harald Klösges, Guido Meßthaler, Michael Keitel, Ralf Landsberg, Gabriele Kasper, Oliver Rauch, Christoph Gatermann, Daniel Ferchland, Gunnar Dennewill

Schönbergstraße 47
73760 Ostfildern (Germany)
T +49.711.342193-0
stuttgart@tmk-architekten.de
www.tmk-architekten.de

→ **178, 194**

tönies + schroeter + jansen freie architekten gmbh
Thomas Jansen, BDA, AKG

Curtiusstraße 19
23568 Lübeck (Germany)
T +49.451.799730
F +49.451.75541
luebeck@tsj-architekten.de
www.tsj-architekten.de

→ **238, 322**

Transsumed GmbH Medizintechnik

Löhrstraße 113
56068 Koblenz (Germany)
T +49.261.1330980
F +49.261.13309812
info@transumed.de
www.transumed.com

→ **154**

Architectenbureau Koen van Velsen

Spoorstraat 69a
1200 BJ Hilversum (The Netherlands)
T +31.35.6222000
F +31.35.6288991
mail@koenvanvelsen.com
www.koenvanvelsen.com

→ **384**

Zeidler Partnership Architects
Jurgen Henze, Alan Munn, Stuart Mussells, Amos Caspi,
Graham Wunsch

315 Queen Street West
M5V 2X2 Toronto (Canada)
T +1.416.5968300
F +1.416.5961408
toronto-info@zeidler.com
www.zeidler.com

→ **22**

The Deutsche Nationalbibliothek lists this publication in
the Deutsche Nationalbibliografie; detailed bibliographic
data are available in the Internet at http://dnb.dnb.de

ISBN 978-3-03768-124-4

© 2013 by Braun Publishing AG
www.braun-publishing.ch

1st edition 2013

Project coordination: Editorial Office van Uffelen
Editorial staff: Maike Müller, Lisa Rogers, Chris van
Uffelen
Graphic concept: ON Grafik | Tom Wibberenz
Layout: Maike Müller, Lisa Rogers
Art direction: Michaela Prinz
Reproduction: Bild1Druck GmbH, Berlin